Lessons from the Heart is a masterpiece. Its biblical teaching, inspirational stories, and passionate encouragement will allow the reader to know Jesus more intimately and develop a heart that beats with the Master.

Neil Clark Warren, Ph.D.
Clinical Psychologist

Jack Graham is a tried and proven minister of the gospel. This choice book reflects his heart for Christ, people, and the gospel. It will bless you richly.

George Sweeting
former Chancellor of the
Moody Bible Institute

Dr. Graham always stimulates your thinking. *Lessons from the Heart* will not only stir your thinking, but will stir your heart. Read it with pleasure and blessing.

Dr. Jerry Vines
Pastor, First Baptist Church,
Jacksonville, Florida

LESSONS
from the
HEART

LEARNING TO
TRUST GOD
FOR TRUE PEACE,
FULFILLMENT
AND JOY

JACK GRAHAM

MOODY PRESS
CHICAGO

All Scripture quotations, unless otherwise indicated, are taken
from the *New King James Version*. Copyright © 1982 by Thomas Nel-
son, Inc. Used by permission. All rights reserved.

Scripture quotations marked KJV are taken from the King James
Version.

Library of Contress Cataloging-in-Publication Data

Graham, Jack, 1950–
    Lessons from the heart : learning to trust God for true peace,
fulfillment, and joy / Jack Graham.
        p. cm.
    Includes bibliographical references.
    ISBN 0-8024-6491-2
    1. Christian life--Baptist authors. I. Title.

BV4501.3 .G73 2001
248.4'861--dc21

2001034503

1 3 5 7 9 10 8 6 4 2

Printed in the United States of America

To my brother,

Robert A. Graham,

*whose godly example and faithful ministry
have inspired and encouraged me
every day of my life.
His loving heart as a pastor, husband, and father
demonstrates the lessons of this book.*

CONTENTS

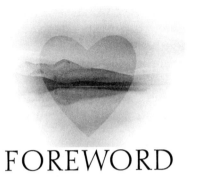

FOREWORD

*A*s a young intern many years ago, I recall distinctly one of my first patients with acute heart disease. He was seen in the emergency room complaining of chest pain and severe shortness of breath. Before we could administer any type of medical treatment (much of which we now use was not available in those days), he suddenly died. Resuscitation was not successful.

Later, the autopsy showed no signs of any heart disease and no coronary artery problems. The final diagnosis was "cardiac arrest." In other words, he died because his heart simply stopped beating.

As the years have gone by, I vividly remember that experience. As our knowledge has increased, and even though a litany of modern techniques is now available to treat cardiac emergencies and we know exactly where the heartbeat comes from, we still do not know what initiates that beat.

With medications, we can slow the heart down or speed it up. Emotional stimuli also can cause it to increase. When the heartbeat stops, at times we can restart it with electrical pacemakers, defibrillators, or certain types of medications. But the fact remains that we still do not know what causes it to originate and, equally as important, what makes it continue to beat at least 10,000 times in a twenty-four-hour period.

According to the psalmist, we are fearfully and wonderfully made (Psalm 139:14), and no organ in the body fits that description better than the heart. You can live with one lung, one kidney, one adrenal gland, and even one-half of your liver, but you cannot live longer than five minutes if your heart stops beating.

Nor can you live abundantly or expect to live eternally unless you have a "heart for the Lord." My pastor, Dr. Jack Graham, describes in *Lessons from the Heart* how to "spiritually condition the heart" as I have told people how to "physically condition the heart," for more than forty years. If you achieve these goals of spiritual and physical fitness, then you have prepared yourself not only for this life but also for the life "which is to come" (1 Timothy 4:8).

KENNETH H. COOPER, M.D.

ACKNOWLEDGMENTS

I want to say a special word of thanks to the people of Prestonwood Baptist Church, whose great heart for God challenges their pastor; to my editor, Philip Rawley, for his significant contribution to this book and the enjoyable conversations about the great game of baseball; to Jim Bell and our friends at Moody Press, for the privilege of publishing with them; and to Dr. Ken Cooper, my physician and friend, for writing the foreword and for helping me keep my heart strong for the work of Christ and His church.

INTRODUCTION

*T*he name Johnny Gruelle is probably not familiar to you. He was born in 1880 and became an accomplished artist, illustrator, and writer. In 1938 Gruelle created a character that has become an important part of Americana ...a yarn-haired rag doll named Raggedy Ann.

The original story of Raggedy Ann centered on the doll's candy heart. Her unique heart made Raggedy Ann different from all the other toys in any child's toy chest.

The subtle truth of this story illustrates the reality that scientists and philosophers have studied for centuries. What is that quality of the human heart that has inspired great discoveries, motivated powerful rulers, and instigated crimes of passion, yet has eluded our complete understanding?

In 1923 Ernest Starling was the first scientist to use the metaphor of wisdom to characterize the heart's quality. He chose Job 38:36: "Who has put wisdom in the mind? Or who has given understanding to the heart?"

It was Aristotle who said, "The heart is the seat of the mind." The heart is so important to the human condition that it takes prominence in most disciplines and studies that attempt to improve the quality of human existence and solve the mystery of life after death.

As Christians we know the importance of our heart in relationship to our salvation because the Bible makes it so very clear that faith begins in the heart.

We have eyes to see, ears to hear, and mouths to speak, but everything they process filters through our hearts. When Jesus was questioned by the lawyers about the greatest commandment, He gave a clear explanation of the strategic position of the heart: "You shall love the Lord your God with all your heart, with all your soul, and with all your mind" (Matthew 22:37).

One of the greatest turnoffs to people who do not know Jesus Christ is a person whose religion is merely external. The Christian life is not a matter of externals, but internals. Unbelievers have a heart cry for genuine spiritual experience and the evidence of that lived out by those professing a "born-again" experience.

We can take medicine to adjust and control almost any bodily function. Our physical health is dependent upon a healthy heart because the blood that flows through the heart carries the necessary elements of life to every cell in the body.

The heart is just as crucial to our spiritual lives. Until a heart has surrendered to the Lord Jesus Christ, a person cannot be complete and truly whole. Without the redeeming love of Christ flowing through a heart, an individual is spiritually dead. However, when the cleansing power of Jesus' blood flows through a heart, the spiritual life flourishes and brings health to every dimension of living.

Our ambitions, affections, and attitudes flow from the motives of our heart. Yet we can know so much by fact and refuse to accept the power to live it out by faith.

Proverbs 16:9 tells us, "A man's heart plans his way, but the Lord directs his steps." The condition of your heart will determine the quality of your spiritual life. I want to help you develop a heart for God that will bring peace, fulfillment, and joy to your life and prepare you to spend eternity with the One who created you.

This is my sole purpose for writing this book. May God bless its message to your heart, and may the truth of His Word become within you "like a burning fire shut up in [your] bones" (Jeremiah 20:9).

Chapter One

THE HEART OF THE MATTER

*I*n his gripping drama *Les Misérables,* French author Victor Hugo tells the story of Jean Valjean, a poor man who served nineteen years in prison at hard labor for the crime of stealing a loaf of bread.

Valjean is finally released from prison and makes his way to the home of a kind bishop. Hardened by his experience, the menacing-looking Valjean is surprised when the bishop serves him a meal, using the bishop's best silver. Then the kindly churchman gives Valjean a bed for the night.

However, the ex-convict is overcome by temptation and desperation. Jean Valjean steals the bishop's silver plates during the night and flees, only to be apprehended by the police, who bring him back to the bishop. Valjean is in despair, knowing he will be returned to the horrors of prison.

But the bishop shocks the police, and Valjean, when he first sees Valjean. "'Ah, there you are!' said he, looking toward Jean Valjean, 'I am glad to see you. But! I gave you the candlesticks also, which are silver like the rest, and would bring two hundred francs. Why did you not take them along with your plates?'"

A stunned Valjean watches as the bishop puts the silver candlesticks in his bag. The police have no choice but to release Valjean, and he goes away a different man. The bishop's act of kindness brings about a change of heart in Jean Valjean, and in true gratitude and repentance he leads a life of kindness and service to others.

Jean Valjean's inner transformation, depicted so powerfully by Victor Hugo, is an example of what I would call a matter of the heart. Matters of the heart are those things that go to the very essence of our being, because the Christian life is designed to be lived from the inside out.

We may be impressed by the way a person looks or dresses, or by some other external factor, but God is interested in the heart. He established this principle when He rejected Eliab, the oldest son of Jesse, as the future king of Israel after Saul's spiritual failure.

The prophet Samuel went to Jesse's house to anoint Israel's next king. When Eliab walked in, Samuel was struck by his appearance. But God told Samuel, "The Lord does not see as man sees; for man looks at the outward appearance, but the Lord looks at the heart" (1 Samuel 16:7). That's why God chose David, "a man after His own heart" (1 Samuel 13:14), as king.

If God is looking this intently at our hearts, then we need to take a very close look at them, too. This is my purpose in the pages that follow. I want to help you put your life under the microscope of God's Word as we learn what the Bible says about our hearts.

We're going to begin our study with Proverbs 3:5–6, a familiar passage of Scripture that has become a life text for me. These verses are a lodestar pointing us in the right direction concerning matters of the heart, because they begin with the ringing declaration "Trust in the Lord with all your heart." If I had to sum up this book in one sentence, this would be my choice. A heart that is fully trusting in the Lord is a heart that will not be easily led astray.

The particular focus of Proverbs 3:5–6 is God's guidance, or His will for our lives. Solomon exhorted us to trust wholly in God, then added, "Lean not on your own understanding; in all your ways acknowledge Him, and He shall direct your paths." These verses contain the promise that God has a purpose for everyone whose trust is in Him. The Scripture teaches that God has a specific, original, unique, and definitive will for every believer's life.

God expresses His will in several ways. He has a sovereign will because He is the Sovereign, or Ruler, of the universe. God's sovereign will is that by which He providentially rules in all the circumstances and conditions of our world. God is sovereignly engaged in our lives because He controls the destiny of every creature in His creation.

It's also true that God has a moral will, given in the commands and precepts of His Word, designed to guide our ethics and behavior. When we talk about seeking God's guidance, we need to remember that much of His will for us is already revealed in the pages of Scripture.

In addition to His sovereign and moral will, God has a specific will for each of us. His plan for you is a good plan, to bring you to salvation and then to bless you along the way with His very best. "I know the thoughts that I think toward you, says the Lord, thoughts of peace and not of evil, to give you a future and a hope" (Jeremiah 29:11).

That's why to know and to do God's will is the greatest privilege of life and the best definition of success I've ever heard. True success comes when you know and follow God's good, perfect, and specific will for your life (see Romans 12:1–2). Don't ever think that God reveals His will only to ministers and missionaries. Whatever your vocation or location, God invites you to seek Him with all your heart and say yes to His best for you. Let's find out what it takes to get to the heart of God's guidance.

LOOK TO THE LORD

You are on your way to discovering God's will for your life when you look to Him in confidence and count on Him for guidance. That's what it means to trust in the Lord. The word *trust* in Proverbs 3:5 literally means to lie facedown. It's the picture of a soldier surrendering to a conqueror or a servant bowing before his master.

When you are bowed down, the only way you can see the face of the person you're bowing to is to look up. When we bow down and look up to God, we are expressing complete, childlike trust.

The Only Sensible Way to Live

Trust is the only way to live. For example, it's the act by which we enter the family of God. In order to be saved from our sins and be assured of heaven, we have to quit trusting in our own goodness or good works to make us acceptable to God. Salvation comes when we transfer our trust to the Lord Jesus Christ and His death, burial, and resurrection for our sins.

Salvation is just the beginning of the Christian life because trust is not only an act, it's an attitude. It is both a point at which we receive Christ and a process by which we grow in Christ. All of life is about learning to trust God in every detail. Christians who don't learn to trust spend their days fretting and fuming and wringing their hands like the children of Israel wandering in the wilderness.

You may be suffering from a loss right now—loss of health, loss of a family member or friend, or a financial loss —and wondering why this is happening. But you can trust that ultimately God is working in you for His best and your best, and you are never outside of His loving presence.

Access to God's Unchangeable Wisdom

When you draw near to God, there is infallible wisdom to direct you, perfect love to keep you, and eternal power to protect you. God's will for His people is not held captive to the ups and downs of human existence.

One of the lasting images I have from the 2000 presidential election night coverage is commentator Tim Russert, who sat in the network control room with his little erasable board and marker, showing the various combinations of state electoral votes that George W. Bush or Al Gore needed to win the White House.

The lineup kept changing throughout the night as the votes came in, and that man's erasable board almost took on a life of its own. We saw how easily one state could turn the entire election around.

This may be the way we elect presidents, but it's not the way God operates His world. He's not sitting in heaven with a marker and an erasable board, changing His plans in response to what happens on earth. Instead, the Bible says, "The eyes of the Lord run to and fro throughout the whole earth, to show Himself strong on behalf of those whose heart is loyal to Him" (2 Chronicles 16:9). It is trust that moves the heart of God.

If you want an exciting adventure, live each day trusting God from your heart. The greatest opportunities in life are given to those who are willing to say, "Lord, my life is Yours. I trust You explicitly and completely. I take my hands off my life. I no longer trust in me, but I trust in You."

I'm not suggesting that we just shove our brains into neutral and coast through life. Proverbs 3:5 does *not* say, "Don't have any understanding." As we experience things along the way, we're certainly to try to discern what God is teaching us and where He's leading us.

But we're not to *trust in* our own understanding. Human ingenuity and resources aren't enough because we will never understand everything. Our challenge is to remember that during those times when we don't see where God is taking us, we can lean on His love and goodness.

That's what it means to look to God in an attitude of complete trust. He's guiding and guarding us all the way. Even when things around us seem unfair and life doesn't seem to have any rhyme or reason, we can trust God to make a way where there is no way.

LEAN ON THE LORD

If you were bowing down before someone in humble submission and looking up to him in complete trust, it would be easy and natural to *lean* on that person if he reached down to you and drew you to himself. That's what God does when we trust in Him, which is why the Scripture invites us to lean on Him instead of on our own meager strength.

There's No Fear When We Lean

But leaning on the Lord demands that we trust Him with *all* of our hearts in *all* of our ways. It's as if we give God a blank check for our lives and say, "Lord, fill in the blanks, because I know You know what is best for me."

I know some Christians are afraid of what God might do with them if they lean on Him in this way. Suppose my son Joshua came to me one day and said, "Dad, I've been thinking. I know you love me and want what's best for me. I also know you're a lot wiser than I am, and you've been down the road farther than I've been. So, Dad, I just want you to know that from now on, I'm going to do my best to obey you and follow your guidance. My goal is to be the son you want me to be."

Now if Joshua came to me with that kind of trust, am I going to respond like this: "Joshua, you'll regret the day you ever said that to me. This is just what I've been waiting for. I'm going to make your life miserable from here on out.

"First of all, no more fun and games. When you come in from school every day, you're going to do nothing but homework until you go to bed. I'm going to get rid of all your sports gear. No more baseball or football. And you're going to eat spinach and green beans at every meal."

Is that what I'm going to say? Of course not! I would probably say, "Hey, Josh, that's great! I want you to know I'm going to do my very best to make sure you never have to regret your decision. Let's go get an ice cream cone and then play some catch and talk about it."

The fact is that I do love Joshua and want the very best for his life. I would do anything necessary to make sure my son had the very best in life. And I assure you, this comes from a father who is selfish and sinful and finite.

But we have a heavenly Father who is not selfish, sinful, or finite, and who loves us more than we can imagine. What do we have to fear from a Father like that? Absolutely nothing!

When you come to God and say, "Here is my life; I trust You completely," He will move heaven and earth if necessary to make sure you receive His best. You can lean fully on the Lord without fear that He will let you fall.

Are You on God's Altar?

Most of us don't discover whether our lives are on God's altar until the tough times hit. I experienced this in a dramatic way several years ago when I had a health problem for the first time in my life.

I've always been healthy, and I stay very active. But all of a sudden I started feeling sick. For about two or three months, I felt like I was seasick all the time. I underwent a series of medical tests, after which the doctors put me in the hospital and took out my gallbladder.

But I still didn't feel any better, so I went back for more extensive tests. These included being enclosed in a very narrow cylinder for an MRI scan. That test was a frightening experience for me. It was like being put on a slab and slid into a mausoleum. In that cylinder I was shut off from everything, lying perfectly still, and unable to hear anything except the loud knocking of that scanner for what seemed like an awfully long time.

I was afraid, but I prayed, "Lord, I'm making this cylinder an altar to You. Whatever the results of this test, good or bad, I want You to know that I'm on the altar. My life is Yours, and I'm trusting You." At that moment an overwhelming sense of peace flooded my heart.

The tests showed nothing seriously wrong, and I've been fine since. But it took some time, and that period of fear and uncertainty was a turning point in my life.

Yes, I had put myself on the altar before. And as far as I knew at the time, I was surrendered to God's will before my health took a turn downward. But I needed the trial of that sickness to make sure my life really was where I said it was. It was good for me to learn that I could lean on God even in the tough times.

I wish I could say that I'm always on the altar. But the problem with a living sacrifice is that it wants to keep crawling off the altar. All of us struggle to stay in the position of complete surrender to and dependence on God. But it is in the arms of God that we find sweet serenity, as He draws us to Himself and we lean on Him.

Don't be afraid to follow the Lord. He has your best interests at heart. Someone said, "God will choose for you what you would choose for yourself if you had sense enough to choose it." Another person put it this way: "The will of God is what you would choose for yourself if you knew all the facts."

We don't have all the facts, and sometimes we just don't have enough sense to make the right choice. So the best thing we can do is lean on the Lord and not on our own understanding. Once we make that full, unconditional surrender of our lives to the Lord, we're ready to hear what He has to say to us.

LISTEN TO THE LORD

When God reaches down to you and draws you to Himself, you're in a good position to hear Him when He speaks to you. "In all your ways acknowledge Him, and He shall direct your paths," the writer of Proverbs tells us (3:6). We need to realize that God is speaking to us and be ready to listen.

It's like the parent who says to a child, "Are you listening to me? Nod your head if you're hearing what I'm saying." God wants us to acknowledge that we're listening to Him, that He has our attention.

How does a person listen to God? It's a lifelong process of learning to be sensitive to the Holy Spirit. Here are some signposts that have helped me discern the voice of God and know I am in His will in the decisions and choices I have to make. I hope they will help point you to the heart of the matter concerning God's guidance.

These are things that will help you no matter what kind of decision you're facing. When I was asked to be the pastor of our church in Dallas, I looked for some signposts to help me know I was on the right path as we weighed the decision to leave Florida and come to Texas. I commend these principles to you and encourage you to make them part of your daily spiritual discipline:

Make a Daily Appointment with God

Don't say you're interested in knowing the will of God if you don't take time on a regular basis to listen to God and seek Him.

Did you know that God is more interested in who you

are than in what you're doing or where you're doing it? It's true. God is about the business of building our character, molding us into the image of Christ. He's looking for people who want to know Him more than they want anything else.

Psalm 37:4 says, "Delight yourself also in the Lord, and He shall give you the desires of your heart." So I advise you to give the very best part of your day to God. For most of us, that means getting up early in the morning to spend time with God before the business of the day crowds in on us.

But if the morning is not your best time, that's fine too. The important thing is to meet God in a quiet time of uninterrupted intimacy and fellowship. Ask Him to speak to you through His Word and by His Spirit as you open your Bible with a heart that's ready to listen.

I would also suggest that you read the Word systematically, so you won't wander around and lose your focus. One of the reasons we don't stay with a quiet time very long is that we decide we're going to read the Bible straight through, from cover to cover. That's a great goal, but it's easy to develop a severe case of "Leviticus-itis" and give up. If you have never had a systematic plan for reading the Word, you may want to start in Matthew 1 and also Psalm 1, and work from there.

The exciting part about getting into the Word regularly is that probably 90 percent of what we need to know about God's will for life is found in the Word. And direction for the other 10 percent of God's will is in His Word too, in the form of a principle or a promise. Nothing can substitute for your daily appointment with God.

Expect Peace and Joy

I often write "Romans 15:13" after my name when I sign a letter or something else. Paul says there, "Now may the God of hope fill you with all joy and peace in believing, that you may abound in hope by the power of the Holy Spirit."

If you are trusting God with all your heart and leaning on Him for your strength, your life will be marked by peace and joy. When you do the will of God, there will be a sense of rightness, of "oughtness," about it.

God's people need to understand that His will is not something we have to do. It's something we *get* to do! There's joy in doing God's will. It's the most exciting adventure in life. So expect peace and joy.

Be Willing to Wait on God

What about those times when there is a check in your spirit, a question mark in your mind, about the right way to go? Then move on to the third signpost: Wait on the Lord.

Too many of us operate by the concept "When in doubt, go ahead." But doubt can be a signal that we should wait. God may want us to wait until we have more insight or information and can make a wise decision. In the meantime, God may be purifying and preparing us for something more and better than we would have if we forged on ahead.

Have you ever thanked God for *not* answering some of those prayers you prayed a long time ago? Remember in high school when you prayed, "O dear God, give me that guy. I just know he's the right one for me"? But you didn't marry him. Then twenty years later you went to your class reunion and saw the guy you once wanted to marry. Then you said, "Thank You, Jesus, for unanswered prayer!" Be willing to wait on God.

Keep Moving Forward

No, this is not a contradiction. Even while you're waiting for guidance on a decision you're still in doubt about, keep on doing the will of God as you know it right now.

The issue in God's will is not so much what you are going to do in the next ten years but what you are going to do in the next ten minutes. We already know so much of God's will, yet we don't always obey what we know. And you can mark it down: God is not going to take us one step farther than the measure of our obedience.

So as you wait on God, don't get caught up in the "paralysis of analysis" and let your walk with God come to a standstill. Keep doing what you know God wants you to do, and He will direct your path in the things you don't know. That's the promise of His Word.

Seek Wise Counsel

When you need guidance, talk to someone who not only knows and loves you but who knows and loves God and whose life is saturated in His Word.

I remember when my wife, Deb, and I were students at Hardin-Simmons University in Abilene, Texas. We were living in married student housing, and I pastored a little church on the weekends for forty dollars a week.

Deb was going to school and working for one of the coaches. I was playing baseball on a scholarship, which provided us with some help on our housing. But things were still tight financially.

We found a little white house with a picket fence that we really liked, but it was about thirty dollars a month more than we were paying for our housing. So we sat down and put the pencil to paper and figured out we could afford the extra thirty dollars a month to get our little white house with a picket fence.

Then Deb's father, who is a wonderful Christian man, came over. I told him about the house and took him to see it. He liked it and agreed that it was a good house for his daughter. I was feeling pretty good at this point, so I showed my father-in-law my financial figures and asked, "Do you think we can do this?"

He looked the paper over for a while. I think he was trying not to offend me, since I was a pastor and all of that. But as he looked at my figures, he said, "Well, Jack, it all looks good except for one thing I don't see here. Maybe you've accounted for it somewhere else, but I don't see your tithe in here."

A warning light immediately went off in my head. Deb's dad was right. It wasn't that I had purposely left out our tithe; I just forgot to include it. But it made all the difference, because we really couldn't afford the house if we were going to honor and obey God by our giving.

Without my father-in-law's wise counsel at that crucial moment, Deb and I might have made a financial decision we couldn't afford, and it would have cost us in our giving. Any decision that causes you to disobey God in some area of your life is the wrong decision.

I had blinders on when I calculated that we could afford that house. It was the wise counsel of an experienced Christian that woke me up and helped me see the reality of the situation. We all have blind spots and need somebody to help us see things through God's eyes.

Be Bold and Take Some Risks

Don't play it safe all your life and then wonder what might have been if you had dared to step out in faith and trust God with all your heart. If He is directing your steps, you won't go astray by boldly following Him. When He shows you an open door, go through it in the name of Jesus!

Are you truly looking to the Lord, leaning on Him, and listening to Him? If so, you are saying yes to His best for your life.

NOTE

1.Victor Hugo, trans. Charles E. Wilbour, *Les Miserables* (New York: Modern Library, n.d.), 89.

Chapter Two

PRESCRIPTION FOR A HEALTHY HEART

*N*ot long ago, the federal government took exception to a food processing company's claim that its packaged chicken deserved the label "heart healthy." The Food and Drug Administration said the product did not meet the approved standards for the "heart healthy" label, and it insisted that the company remove this designation from its packaging.

People may wonder how they can know for sure which foods promote a healthy heart when the experts can't even agree. But we don't have this problem in the spiritual realm. God has given us His divine formula for a healthy spiritual heart, and we can trust His Word completely when it tells us how to enjoy "heart healthy" living.

Hundreds of times in both Testaments Scripture refers to the human heart, the totality of who and what we are inside. Biblically, the heart is the seat of our thinking, our emotions, and our character, that part of us called our personality. What we feel and what we think are issues of the heart.

The ancient Hebrews believed that the heart was the center of reflection and contemplation, the place where life's great issues were resolved. That's why the writer of Proverbs said, "As [a person] thinks in his heart, so is he" (23:7).

The importance of the heart also explains why the Bible cautions, "Keep your heart with all diligence, for out of it spring the issues of life" (Proverbs 4:23). It's obvious that we need to pay attention to our hearts, so I want to take you to a familiar New Testament chapter that contains a dynamic prescription for a healthy heart.

Verses 4–9 of Philippians 4 should have a heart symbol beside them in the margin, the way some restaurants put little symbols beside certain items on the menu to indicate they are heart healthy. The key in this passage is what the Bible calls peace, which means far more than simply the absence of conflict. The Hebrew term *shalom* means well-being or wholeness, a sense of being together at the center of life.

World leaders and ordinary people just trying to make it to Friday have something in common. They all have to deal with the anxiety, trouble, and stress of life at some level.

In the midst of these trials, we need to know the peace that can only be found when we are heart healthy in Jesus Christ. At least six principles in Philippians 4:4–9 make up God's prescription for a healthy heart. These truths are even more remarkable because they come from a prison cell, not from the pastor's study. The apostle Paul wrote the letter to the Philippians while he was in chains, facing death for the cause of Christ and the gospel.

Being a prisoner of the Roman Empire was hardly conducive to good physical health and long life. But Paul's heart was healthy, and his spirit was free, because he was properly aligned with God's purposes for his life.

How else can we explain the fact that a man whose

head could have been on the chopping block any day could write, "Be anxious for nothing" (Philippians 4:6)? Someone who can display peace and poise in the face of death has something important to teach us. What are the principles that can make us spiritually heart healthy?

THE PRINCIPLE OF CELEBRATION

"No matter what your circumstances, no matter what prison walls you may face, rejoice in all things." This was Paul's message throughout the book of Philippians. "Rejoice in the Lord always. Again I will say, rejoice!" (Philippians 4:4).

Paul was a seasoned, scarred veteran of many wars for Christ. And yet he was not cynical or calloused. His life was a continual feast of joy. His great spirit was undaunted.

Jesus told His disciples the night before He was crucified, "These things I have spoken to you, that My joy may remain in you, and that your joy may be full" (John 15:11). When your joy is in Jesus, it remains forever.

If your joy is in your possessions, those things could disappear and your joy would be gone. If your joy is in your health, your health may dissipate and your joy will evaporate with it. Even if your joy is in your family and friends, they can be taken away. But when your joy is in Jesus, not even prison or a cross can take it away. That's the joy Paul was talking about.

Christian joy is not just a temporary mood or an emotion. It is often contrasted to happiness, which by definition depends on what happens. If it just so happens that what happens to you makes you happy, then you'll be happy. But that process can be reversed in a minute.

However, biblical joy is something that comes from deep within. The Scripture says, "The joy of the Lord is your strength" (Nehemiah 8:10). We need to learn to enjoy the Lord more and complain about our circumstances less.

I don't know who decided long ago that Christians should look as if they swallowed the Communion rail. My boyhood pastor used to say some Christians look like they were weaned on a dill pickle.

That's bad advertising for the faith. Our lives ought to be marked by genuine, lasting, living joy. There's a peaceful, gentle quality to this joy, because we know "the Lord is at hand" (Philippians 4:5). Focusing on Christ and His soon return has a wonderful way of helping us sort out what is really important. And in the light of heaven, we soon learn that there's really not that much worth getting upset about on earth.

THE PRINCIPLE OF ELIMINATION

Since Christ can return at any time, we really don't have time to sweat the small stuff. Paul addressed worry by saying simply, "Be anxious for nothing" (Philippians 4:6).

Worry is a problem for a lot of people. In fact, some of us worry when we don't have anything to worry about. And it's not just a problem for people outside the church. Worry can wear out believers too; all of us fight the battle.

The word *worry* in Scripture means "to be divided." It's having your mind and your heart torn apart. The old Saxon word for worry, *wurgen,* described a wolf grabbing a sheep by the throat and strangling it. What a picture!

Worry will choke you physically. We know that all kinds of physical illnesses and disabilities are a direct result of stress and worry. If you want an *un*healthy heart, make fretting a way of life.

Worry will also strangle us emotionally, depleting our energy. But worry is a spiritual problem too, because in effect it slanders every promise in the Word of God. We need to know that, for us as believers, worry is not just a weakness. It's not just human nature. Worry is a sin against God.

To worry is to say, "Lord, I don't think You're big

enough to handle this one." Worry divides and distracts us, forcing us to take our attention off the right things.

Someone has said, "Where worry begins, faith ends." Faith is the antidote for anxiety. If you're an anxiety addict, the Bible's word to you is to replace worry with trust. Otherwise, you'll spend all of your time and energy on issues that don't matter all that much in the end.

One of my favorite stories along this line involves a lonely widow whose friends advised her to get a pet. So she went down to the pet store, not sure what kind of pet to buy. The store owner suggested a talking parrot. "This parrot is a talking machine," he told her. "He'll talk to you, and you won't be lonely."

So the woman bought the parrot. But after a few weeks, she became concerned because the parrot wasn't talking. She went back to the store and told the owner, "My parrot isn't talking."

"Well, is he looking in his little mirror?" the owner asked.

"What mirror?"

"Oh," he said, "parrots like to look at themselves in a mirror. When they see themselves, they feel good and start talking."

So the woman bought a little mirror and put it in the parrot's cage. But the bird still wouldn't talk, so after a week or so she headed back to the pet store and reported her problem.

"I can't believe it," the owner said. "Is your parrot climbing up and down his little ladder?"

"What ladder?"

"Why, your parrot will never talk unless he has a little ladder to exercise on. Get him a ladder to go with his mirror, and he'll talk your head off." So the woman dutifully bought a ladder and put it in the cage.

But after two weeks passed and the bird still wouldn't talk, the lonely widow trudged back to the pet store. By now she was a little perturbed. "This parrot hasn't made a peep!"

The store owner was perplexed too. Finally, he asked, "Is the bird swinging on his little swing?"

You know what the woman said. "What swing?"

"Well, there's your problem. A parrot has to swing on his swing and go up and down his ladder and look in his mirror if he's going to talk."

"Give me the swing!" the woman demanded. She bought the swing and put it in the cage—but the bird still wouldn't talk. In fact, two weeks later it died! Now the woman was really angry. She stormed into the pet store and said, "My parrot died!"

The owner was stunned. "Did he ever say anything?"

"Well, as a matter of fact he did. In his dying breath he squawked, 'Don't they have any food at that pet store?'"

That's the way we live sometimes. We're so busy filling our lives with the mirrors, ladders, and swings that we forget to feed our souls.

Worry is wasteful. It never solved a problem or dried a tear. Ninety percent of the things we worry about never happen anyway. Or we worry about things we can't change.

The lesson we need to learn from the heart of God is to rejoice in everything and worry about nothing. The psalmist said, "I sought the Lord, and He heard me, and delivered me from all my fears" (Psalm 34:4).

Christians are not immune from worry. The upright can get uptight. But instead of allowing yourself to be gripped by worry, put yourself in the grip of God's grace.

THE PRINCIPLE OF INVOCATION

The Scripture commands us to pray instead of being anxious. "In everything by prayer and supplication, with thanksgiving, let your requests be made known to God; and the peace of God, which surpasses all understanding, will guard your hearts and minds through Christ Jesus" (Philippians 4:6–7).

In prayer we reach down to the deepest desires, needs, and concerns of our hearts. One poll indicated that more than 80 percent of Americans pray at least on a weekly basis. I wonder what the same survey would reveal about Christians. We believe in prayer, but do we pray?

I'm not talking about the kind of prayer a soldier prayed in his foxhole as enemy bullets were flying overhead. He prayed, "Lord, if You'll get me out of this one, I'll never bother You again."

Real prayer is not an emergency flare we shoot to light up the sky when we're in trouble so God can find us and rescue us. Paul was writing about an intimate, day-by-day communion and conversation with God. Prayer is as much an expression of devotion and trust as it is the voicing of our requests.

But please notice that God *does* invite us to bring Him our requests. Someone may say, "Does that mean we can ask God for anything at all?"

No, there's an important condition to our asking. "Delight yourself also in the Lord, and He shall give you the desires of your heart" (Psalm 37:4). A spiritually healthy heart is so closely attuned to God's heart that we want for ourselves what He wants for us.

God does not always change our circumstances when we pray. But I know that when I pray God begins to change me, which is often far more important than changing my circumstances.

If the only time I can know joy and peace is when good things happen to me, I'm in trouble, because the events of my life can change from good to bad in a moment. But if my joy and serenity come from within . . . if God changes *me* . . . then ultimately it doesn't matter whether I'm in prison or in prosperity.

Prayer puts us in a position of humility to hear from

God and receive what He has for us. That's where the peace comes.

Sometimes I think we fall into the mind-set of the man who was in deep trouble when someone suggested that he pray. "Good grief!" he cried. "Has it come to that?"

For the world, prayer may be a last, desperate resort. But for God's people, prayer is the place to start. We tend to say, "Why pray about it when you can worry about it?" But God says, "Don't worry about it when you can pray about it." Prayer is a powerful weapon greater than your fears or problems. It is listening to and talking with your Creator and Redeemer. So pray about everything.

THE PRINCIPLE OF ADORATION

Thanksgiving may be only one day a year on the world's calendar. But for those of us who know the Lord, thanksgiving is to become thanks*living*. The Bible says we are to pray "with thanksgiving" (Philippians 4:6).

Saying "Thank you" for a gift or favor doesn't come hard to most people. But living with a spirit of gratitude is another story altogether. The grace of God has to become operative in our hearts before we can say with conviction, "I will bless the Lord at all times; His praise shall continually be in my mouth" (Psalm 34:1).

Praise is not only "beautiful" for the upright (Psalm 33:1); it's also the unmistakable mark of a believer. If you want an eye-opening study, trace the words "thanks" or "thanksgiving" through Paul's writings and see how much gratitude is part of what it means to be a Christian.

When thanksgiving becomes a way of life and the first thing that comes out of our mouths, we can thank God in any circumstance. In fact, this is His revealed will for us. "In everything give thanks; for this is the will of God in Christ Jesus for you" (1 Thessalonians 5:18).

When we pray with a spirit of genuine gratitude and adoration to God in everything, our praise produces peace. Why? Because God inhabits the praises of His people (see Psalm 22:3). God comes among us in a powerful way when we thank and praise Him. He draws near to us when we pour out the gratitude of our hearts to Him. When we lift Him up, we are lifted up into His presence.

How can we be thankful for everything? Because we know that God will never allow anything to happen to us that's outside of His perfect will. That's why Jesus taught us to pray, "Your will be done" (Matthew 6:10), and why He prayed the same for Himself as He faced the cross (Matthew 26:39).

Aleksandr Solzhenitsyn was a Russian army officer when he was arrested on trumped-up charges by the Soviet Communist regime and sent to a Siberian labor camp for eleven years. Solzhenitsyn later exposed the horrors of that system in his disturbing book *The Gulag Archipelago.*

Those prisoners suffered in ways beyond our imagination. But Solzhenitsyn could also write, "Thank you, prison cell," for it was through his ordeal that Aleksandr Solzhenitsyn met Jesus Christ and his life was changed forever.

When we ask God to accomplish His "good and acceptable and perfect will" in our lives (Romans 12:2), we can thank Him for everything He sends us—even prison.

THE PRINCIPLE OF CONCENTRATION

It is difficult to think two thoughts at the same time. That means if I am thinking about right things, I won't be concentrating on wrong things.

Guarding what we think about is another important element in the prescription for a healthy heart. Paul gave us a wonderful formula for thinking right thoughts. "Finally, brethren, whatever things are true, whatever things are noble, whatever things are just, whatever things are pure, whatever things are lovely, whatever things are of good report, if there is any virtue and if there is anything praiseworthy—meditate on these things" (Philippians 4:8).

You can't always control the thoughts that pass through your mind, but God can help you to control your thought life by focusing your attention on what is noble and lovely and pure.

Fifteen college professors were once challenged to study all the books they could find on the subject of motivation and then summarize the books in one statement. Here's what these professors came up with: "What the mind attends to, it considers. What the mind does not attend to, it dismisses. What the mind attends to continually, it believes. What the mind believes, it eventually does."

That's a formula we can trace in Scripture. The psalmist advised, "Be angry, and do not sin. Meditate within your heart on your bed, and be still" (Psalm 4:4).

In other words, banish angry, anxiety-producing, sinful thoughts from your mind and heart before you retire for the night. Replace them with positive, inspiring, faith-building thoughts.

Thinking about things that are true and noble and pure takes some effort, because our culture wants to fill our minds with everything that is false and base and degraded. The airwaves are polluted with trash, which is why one of the best things we can do to elevate our thinking is to turn off the tube and open the Book. If you want a healthy heart, think about the right things.

This isn't just self-talk, or hypnosis, or behavior modification. This is concentrating and meditating upon the Word of God, filling our hearts and minds with His truth.

When you think on God's promises and store His Word in your heart through reading, meditation, and memorization, the Holy Spirit can recall those truths to your mind at the exact moment you need them. Many believers can remember the Bible stories they learned in Sunday school or at their father's knee—which is why I hope the Scriptures are at the center of your home.

Memorizing and meditating upon the Word is not just

a helpful exercise. It will keep you from sin. "Your word I have hidden in my heart, that I might not sin against You" (Psalm 119:11).

We're told that we never really forget anything we have seen or heard or read. If you fill your mind and heart with the Word of God, He will bring those true and noble and pure things to your memory.

THE PRINCIPLE OF DEDICATION

The right kind of thinking ought to lead us to the right kind of doing.

There's a marvelous balance to the Word of God. Paul wasn't a mystic sitting under a tree, thinking great thoughts while the world crumbled around his ears. He could write with conviction, "The things which you learned and received and heard and saw in me, these do, and the God of peace will be with you" (Philippians 4:9).

Most of us have had more than our share of "Do as I say, not as I do" role models. But Paul could point to his life and say, "Do as I do. Pour yourself out in ministry."

We've learned that to enjoy spiritually healthy hearts, we need to banish worry and replace fretting with the peace of God. Paul said that God-honoring work is the cure for worry. I've known a lot of people who died of worry, but I've known very few who died of work.

We were created to serve God and to imitate Him in productive work. We enjoy "the peace of God" when we trust Him (Philippians 4:7), and we enjoy the abiding presence of "the God of peace" Himself when we serve Him.

James said, "Be doers of the word, and not hearers only" (James 1:22). Jesus said in John 13:17, "If you know these things, blessed are you if you do them." This is God's psychiatry. Do the right things—and when you do, as Paul said, God's peace will be there to guard (literally, "do sentry duty around") your heart. Paul had an illustration standing right beside him as he wrote. He was being guarded by a

Roman soldier, so he described God's peace as a sentinel walking guard duty around our hearts, providing security and protection.

Jesus said to His worried and fretful disciples in the Upper Room, "Peace I leave with you, My peace I give to you; not as the world gives do I give to you. Let not your heart be troubled, neither let it be afraid" (John 14:27). This is God's peace.

In the Bible you will often see the words *grace* and *peace* coupled together, in that order (see Romans 1:7 as an example). The order is important because you'll never know the peace of God until you experience the grace of God in salvation by putting your faith in Jesus Christ.

Near the end of his life, the great naturalist and writer Henry David Thoreau was urged to make his peace with God. Thoreau replied, "I did not know that we had ever quarreled." That was a clever answer, but the fact is that God does have a "quarrel" with the human race. The reason is called sin, and the reality is that we are all born with hearts that are in rebellion against God. That's why Jesus said, "You must be born again" (John 3:7).

When we receive Jesus Christ as Lord and Savior, by His grace the penalty of sin is paid and we are brought into peace with God. Jesus paid the price so we could enjoy the peace that comes with knowing our sins are forgiven and we are right with God. After He had paid the price for sin and rose from the dead, Jesus appeared to His disciples and said, "Peace to you!" (John 20:26).

If you have never received Jesus Christ as your Savior, you will never know the peace we are talking about. Becoming a Christian is the first step in having a healthy heart.

If you know Christ and yet your life is being choked by stress and worry and the cares of living, I urge you to examine your heart with God's Word open before you. He wants you to begin enjoying heart-healthy living.

Chapter Three

GUARD
YOUR
HEART

A man in the Northeast brought five art glass vases to be appraised at one of those traveling antique shows that are broadcast on many public television stations. The vases had come into this man's possession from a relative's estate. He didn't seem excited about the pieces, even though they carried the name "Tiffany" on their bases. He even called them ugly.

If you know anything about Tiffany glass, you can probably guess what happened. The appraiser confirmed that all five pieces were genuine, the work of the famous art glass designer Louis C. Tiffany. The expert placed their collective value at $13,000, including $3,000–$4,000 apiece for the two larger vases.

Even then, the man acted rather blasé, showing little reaction or emotion. But it was obvious he was surprised at the value of the vases.

This man's reaction was a sharp contrast to an earlier program on which a mother and daughter brought a

Tiffany lamp for appraisal. They knew the lamp was special, and as the appraiser raved about its perfect condition they got more and more excited.

The appraiser finally asked the women if they had any idea of the lamp's value, but they just grabbed each other and held on breathlessly. When he announced that their lamp would probably sell for between $85,000 and $125,000 at auction, the mother burst into tears. She looked as if she were going to faint.

The difference between these events is obvious. The lamp owners knew they had something very precious, and they acted accordingly.

You and I are also in possession of something extremely valuable, even if we're not fully aware of its value. That precious possession is our heart, which in the Bible stands for all that we are in the inner life. When you lay your head on your pillow at night and it's just you and your thoughts, that's when your heart is revealed.

Your heart is your most private world, the place where you feel and dream and make decisions and meditate on eternal things. Your heart was made for God.

We have a divine appraisal of the heart's incredible value in Proverbs 4:23: "Keep your heart with all diligence, for out of it spring the issues of life." The word *keep* here means to exercise great care, to protect something that is valuable, to guard that which is precious.

A good example is a new set of parents bringing their first child home from the hospital. I remember that time well. The idea of being a parent was pretty scary, especially when we weren't exactly sure what we were supposed to do.

When Deb and I brought our son Jason home, sometimes we would just stand guard over the crib, looking at this amazing life God had given us. Or in the middle of the night, we would go check on Jason just to make sure he was still breathing.

Why? Because each child is precious. It doesn't matter

whether our children are in the crib, in college, or in a career. They're still incredibly valuable, and we do everything we can to guard and keep them.

Parents' concern for their children is also a good illustration of what it means to guard our hearts, because Proverbs 4 is part of Solomon's heart-to-heart talk with his son. Through this passage God the Father is saying to His children, "Don't be enticed and misled by the world. Guard your heart."

Christian artist Steve Green expresses this truth in a powerful way:

> *Guard your heart,*
> *Guard your heart.*
> *Don't trade it for pleasure,*
> *Don't give it away.*
> *Guard your heart,*
> *Guard your heart.*
> *As a payment for pleasure,*
> *It's a high price to pay.*
> *For a soul that remains sincere,*
> *with a conscience that's clear,*
> *Guard your heart.*[1]

KEEPING THE THORNS PULLED OUT

In His parable of the sower, Jesus described a group of people whose hearts He characterized as "thorns." These are people who hear the Word of God but allow "the cares of this world, the deceitfulness of riches, and the desires for other things" to choke out the Word so that their lives become unfruitful (Mark 4:19).

This is why we must constantly guard our hearts against the growth of spiritual thorns that can strangle the life of God within us. Let's talk about some of these thorns we need to protect our hearts against.

Don't Let Greed Choke You

There's nothing wrong with making money and earning a living. The Bible says it is God who gives us the power to get wealth (Deuteronomy 8:18). But your heart is greater and more valuable than any material possession.

Jesus gave us this powerful warning in Luke 12:15: "Take heed and beware of covetousness," which is materialism or greed. A greedy spirit can develop in a hurry, because money has a way of deceiving us into thinking that it's all we need.

Jesus followed His warning with the parable of the rich, greedy farmer (Luke 12:16–21). This successful businessman set his heart on his wealth and ended up having to face the God he had ignored.

The Scripture says, "The love of money is a root of all kinds of evil" (1 Timothy 6:10). Paul didn't say that money itself is evil but that it tends to exert a downward pull on our hearts. This pull was illustrated in a fascinating George Gallup survey that asked participants what effect money has on a person's spirituality. Among people who reported making more than $50,000 a year, 62 percent said money caused their spiritual lives to decline. Only 25 percent of this group said money promoted spiritual growth.

Be on Guard Against Phony Faith

Every brand of non-Christian religion, whatever name you care to give it, is spelled d-o . . . *do*. Do this and you'll make it to heaven. Obey these rules and God will accept you. Keep this commandment and you're home free.

In contrast, faith in Jesus Christ is spelled d-o-n-e ...
done. Jesus declared from the cross, "It is finished!" (John
19:30). He took our judgment for sin upon Himself on the
cross and paid the penalty for us. Our loving faith response
is to receive the gift God has given us.

What I call "phony faith" is dangerous to the heart because it is so similar to the real thing. Jesus focused the issue for us when He said, "Take heed and beware of the
leaven of the Pharisees and the Sadducees" (Matthew
16:6).

The Pharisees and Sadducees were the religious elite
of their day—the teachers and biblical scholars who had
all the answers and commanded respect. But they had a religion without a relationship with God. How else could
they argue with Jesus over points of the Mosaic Law, and
then go away and plot to kill Him?

These outwardly righteous leaders wrapped themselves in a cloak of religious legalism and rule-keeping to
hide the fact that their hearts were not right with God. No
one could really tell that by looking at them, because phony faith is so similar to the real thing. That's what makes it
so dangerous. Don't let empty religion take root in your
heart.

Don't Fight; Take Flight

Sexual temptation is so powerful that the only way to
deal with it effectively is to run the other way. It's worth
noting that after telling us to guard our hearts, the writer
of Proverbs devoted the entire fifth chapter to a warning
against allowing ourselves to be led into sexual sin.
Solomon cautioned his son concerning the immoral
woman, "Remove your way far from her" (v. 8). Why? Because sexual sin destroys both body and spirit.

Paul put it more bluntly: "Flee sexual immorality" (1 Corinthians 6:18; see 2 Timothy 2:22). We can't keep our

guard up if we are going to expose ourselves to an assault from the Enemy. God will always provide us with a "back door" of escape if we're looking for it (see 1 Corinthians 10:13). He has also given us the safe haven of marriage for the legitimate expression of sexual desire (Proverbs 5:15–19).

Don't Let Your Life Go up in Smoke

Several things can happen when we fail to take care of our hearts. The apostle John wrote, "Look to yourselves, that we do not lose those things we worked for, but that we may receive a full reward" (2 John 8).

John was not talking about losing our salvation but our reward, the "Well done" from the Father. The Bible teaches that it's possible to see our life's work burned up even while we are saved, "yet so as through fire" (1 Corinthians 3:10–15). This is the picture of a person who barely escapes the flames of hell, but has nothing to show for his or her life.

Besides a loss of reward in the future, failing to guard our hearts is also costly in the present. Many people disqualify themselves from spiritual service and usefulness to the Lord because they didn't take care of business on the inside.

All of us are spiritual examples at some level. We all exercise spiritual influence in someone else's life, even when we may not be aware of it. If we fail to take care of our hearts, we forfeit our right to lead.

You may be thinking, *But what about forgiveness?* Of course, forgiveness is available to anyone who falls into sin. After King David had committed adultery with Bathsheba and covered it up for a year, he finally and fully repented, and God forgave him (2 Samuel 11–12). David retained his throne, but the rest of 2 Samuel records that his kingdom went downhill from that day forward. David also suffered damage to his inner person and his family that he never completely recovered from.

So even though a sinning believer can be forgiven and restored, escaping without damage and regaining one's spiritual influence is another issue. Failing to guard your heart can cause you to forfeit your leadership for days, months, or years—or maybe even a lifetime.

Now in case you're beginning to think that spiritual failure is somehow inevitable, here's a word of encouragement. For the most part, spiritual failures do not appear suddenly out of nowhere. Instead, people have moral earthquakes because they have secret faults lying below the surface that they've been nurturing for years.

So by tending to your heart and guarding your spiritual life, you can prevent those secret cracks in your character that break through to the surface as moral earthquakes.

A STRATEGIC PLAN FOR GUARDING YOUR HEART

So how do you go about guarding your heart? Here's a basic five-point biblical plan that will help you live a life that pleases the Lord.

Purpose in Your Heart to Live a Pure Life

The problem with so many of us is that we live by our preferences and prejudices rather than by biblical convictions.

Our prejudices and preferences can be compromised and changed, and often should be, but not our convictions about right and wrong based on Scripture. We must purpose down deep to say yes to righteousness and no to sin.

When we do this, some decisions are made for us. The Bible says of Daniel, a new captive of the Babylonian king Nebuchadnezzar, "Daniel purposed in his heart that he would not defile himself with the portion of the king's delicacies, nor with the wine which he drank; therefore he requested of the chief of the eunuchs that he might not defile himself" (Daniel 1:8).

Daniel was being offered the best of Babylon, which

was a lot considering that the Babylonian kingdom was the greatest empire of its day. But Daniel had an entirely different set of priorities.

The king's food had already been offered to Babylonian deities, which would have put Daniel in conflict with God's law if he had eaten (see Exodus 34:15). Therefore, Daniel had a life-shaping choice to make—and he decided to follow the Word, not the world.

Daniel asked for vegetables and water for himself and his friends, and at the end of the testing period they were in better shape than the young captives who compromised and ate the king's food.

The impressive thing to me is that Daniel was a teenager when he was deported to Babylon. And yet Daniel dared to be different, rather than be absorbed into the pagan system of which he was now a part. His faith in God was so strong that he made a decision for integrity that would last his entire lifetime.

I believe Daniel decided in his heart to obey God before he ever left Israel for Babylon. That's the key to this principle. The time to decide whether you're going to live in moral and spiritual purity is not when you're under temptation and the pressure is on. You need to decide in advance to be obedient to God.

Daniel's commitment was so rock-solid that he was still serving the Lord when he was ninety years old. And even then, his obedience got him thrown in a den of lions (Daniel 6)!

But God vindicated His servant once again. Daniel thrived under several different kingdoms and rulers, but it all started as a young man when he made that determined, daring decision in his heart.

Have you said in your heart, "God being my help and His grace being my strength, from this day forward I purpose to live a pure life"? God blessed Daniel for making this decision, and God will bless you for the righteous decisions you make.

These priority commitments have a wonderful way of clarifying other issues. I am committed to being true to the Lord and faithful to my family, so I don't have to keep making up my mind about these things every time they come around.

Certainly no one is above falling or failing. However, we don't have to be thrown for a loop by every provocation or temptation that comes along. Every time you say yes to Christ and no to temptation, your commitment is strengthened, your character is built, and your heart is made warm toward God.

Make it your passion, your heart's deepest desire, to be pure before the Lord.

Prepare for Ambush

Satan rarely comes at us with a full frontal assault. More often, he ambushes us when we least expect it. He knows where we are the weakest, and that's often the area where he aims his attack. Satan may also hit us where we think we're the strongest and, therefore, not as readily on guard against his assaults.

That's why it is vital that you know your vulnerabilities, so you can expect, detect, and deflect the attacks of the Enemy of your soul. Post a sentinel in those areas where you are most susceptible to attack. This could involve memorizing Scripture, finding an accountability partner, or even something as simple as changing your routine so you avoid certain places or people.

Proverbs 4:24–27 is packed with good advice to help us prepare for ambush. "Put away from you a deceitful mouth, and put perverse lips far from you" (v. 24). In other words, don't let other people lie to you, and don't lie to yourself. So many times we end up compromising our convictions because we listen to the lies about what's right and wrong, or we listen to ourselves negotiate the terms of our commitment. Be honest with yourself and honest with God.

"Let your eyes look straight ahead, and your eyelids look right before you" (Proverbs 4:25). A person who is focused on the path ahead is not easily distracted by side issues.

Many of us sang this little song as children: "Oh, be careful little eyes what you see." That's good theology! Job said, "I have made a covenant with my eyes; why then should I look upon a young woman?" (Job 31:1). This is the long, lustful look that every man can identify with. The look may be different for women, but all of us have the responsibility to guard ourselves.

Our eyes are the windows to our souls. Advertisers understand the power of visual effects to capture people and prompt them to respond. Companies pay outrageous amounts of money for a thirty-second commercial during a major event such as the Super Bowl, because they're banking on the power of their images to connect with viewers.

Unfortunately, the peddlers of sexual filth also understand the importance of the eyes. These people know how to entice their victims through what they see on television, at the movies, or on videos in a hotel room. If you aren't on guard about what passes before your eyes and goes down into your heart, you are sowing dangerous seeds that will yield a bitter harvest.

I know a great Christian leader who drapes a towel over the television set whenever he stays in a hotel room. Then he places his Bible on top of the towel, and a picture of his family on top of the Bible, just for good measure. That's a great idea. Maybe we should start an accountability group for Christian men called "The Company of the Towel." Do whatever it takes to help you guard your heart.

We have another tool to help us in the battle with our sex-saturated culture. It's called the remote control—with the emphasis on *control*. That little piece of technology works very well when something comes on television that you or your children shouldn't be watching. Just turn it off.

Let's not kid ourselves. We have a lot of control over what goes into our minds and hearts. Some Christians are allowing moral cesspools to discharge filth into their homes via cable or satellite television channels.

You wouldn't pay someone to come into your home and spread garbage around, so why let purveyors of moral garbage come in and spread their filth? The best exchange we can make is to replace what is vile and unwholesome with that which is pure and holy (see Philippians 4:8).

"Don't listen to lies" and "watch your eyes" are two pieces of invaluable advice. Here's a third, from Proverbs 4:26: "Ponder the path of your feet, and let all your ways be established." Don't go anywhere mentally or visually that you have no business going, and don't go there physically either.

I think of Joseph, who ran out of his master Potiphar's house after he ran into temptation with Potiphar's wife (Genesis 39:7–12). Joseph didn't negotiate or debate with her. He didn't start a Bible study or witness to her. He just got into Potiphar's chariot and ran from the woman's moral ambush.

We have a major problem today that makes it much more difficult for us to keep our hearts pure, and that is our society's incredibly loose attitude toward sin. This expresses itself in everything from pornography to "reality television."

In earlier generations, the prevailing belief in the public square was that morality was right and immorality was wrong. But today, instead of condemning immorality, we have TV programs that set up immoral situations and then invite people to sin while the nation watches.

One difference between Joseph's day and ours is that, more than likely, today Potiphar's wife and a film crew would have agreed ahead of time to seduce Joseph, and a hidden camera would have been there to capture the scene. That's not far-fetched, because that's exactly what happened to the husband of a well-known TV personality a few years ago. He was set up by a tabloid magazine that hired a woman to seduce him. Unfortunately, he fell into the trap.

Entrapment is not an excuse for sin, but it's still a dirty trick. Joseph was entrapped in the sense that Potiphar's wife waited for just the right moment and cornered him. But Joseph knew what to do with his feet, and he found that way of escape that God always provides.

An old saying warns, "He who would not fall down should not walk in slippery places." Ponder the path of your feet. Don't turn to the right or the left. You're less likely to be ambushed if you stay on the path God has marked out for you in His Word.

Practice Dynamic Spiritual Disciplines

Don't just deny your heart what is unhealthy, but fill it with what is healthy. I'm really encouraged to see a resurgence of interest in the practice of spiritual disciplines such as prayer, fasting, and worship among God's people.

Many of us are just now discovering what believers of old have known for centuries. A fulfilling, God-honoring spiritual life doesn't just happen willy-nilly. It's the result of disciplined, regular spiritual exercise, just as surely as a healthy body is the result of regular physical exercise.

Paul told Timothy, "Bodily exercise profits a little, but godliness is profitable for all things" (1 Timothy 4:8). There is tremendous profit, for example, in fasting as a means of laying aside food or some other material comfort to focus on the Lord.

Prayer retreat centers have also become very popular in recent years. One such center in France regularly draws thousands of visitors, including teenagers. These are not retreats as we think of them, but places devoted primarily to teaching believers how to develop disciplined prayer lives and deepen their worship.

There's no doubt that the church needs this. A pastor who has visited several of these prayer centers in Europe said, "As a pastor and a Christian, I have been especially concerned about the inadequacy of most Christian prayer for a culture in which many are formed by a weekly average of 28 hours of television."[2]

Regular study of and meditation on Scripture is also a necessary spiritual discipline. It's so important that we as Christians know what we believe. Can I say that many professing Christians are theologically challenged? They don't know what they believe, so every wind of false doctrine that blows knocks them off their feet.

When we know who we are in Christ and what His Word teaches, we are much more proficient and powerful in counteracting the lies that Satan and the world throw at us.

Guarding your heart involves developing the spiritual maturity to discipline yourself in godliness. Do you have a daily time with God in which you feed upon His Word? Are you disciplining yourself in prayer? There is no easy way to achieve maturity or spiritual character.

The psalmist said, "Delight yourself also in the Lord, and He shall give you the desires of your heart" (Psalm 37:4). Ask God to give you desires that are godly and beneficial, to transform your thinking, and to renew your mind (see Romans 12:2).

If you feed your heart with Scripture, prayer, praise, and worship, you can reprogram your outlook on life. But you have to be willing to pay the price of being spiritually disciplined.

Weigh the Devastating Consequences of Failure

Just as a thief looks for unlocked and unguarded doors, there's nothing Satan loves to see more than an unlocked heart.

Proverbs 7:7–23 is a powerful description of a foolish young man who is enticed by a prostitute. He follows her without thinking about the consequences, and he is led to destruction "as an ox goes to the slaughter" (v. 22). Think about the damage that will be done if you let down your guard.

One of the things that keeps me serious about protecting my heart is the realization that years of service for the Lord could be washed away by one foolish act. When I think about the damage that my failure would do to God's name and the devastation it would bring to my family and others, it puts me on my knees.

We need to be like Paul, who said, "I discipline my body and bring it into subjection, lest, when I have preached to others, I myself should become disqualified" (1 Corinthians 9:27). Paul didn't want to be benched, put on the shelf, no longer usable for the kingdom of God. Weigh the issues involved, and you'll see that there's too much at stake to let down your guard.

Partner with Other Believers

There is no such thing in Scripture as a believer living in isolation—at least not successfully. You don't have to go it alone in living the Christian life. In fact, I strongly urge you not to try to go it alone. Become accountable to another believer or other believers who will hold you up in prayer, strengthen you, and tell you the truth in love when you need it.

As Christians, we are members of the body of Christ (see 1 Corinthians 12:12–27). We're so interconnected that "if one member suffers, all the members suffer with it; or if one member is honored, all the members rejoice with it" (v. 26). None of us can say to other believers, "I don't need you."

Partnering with other Christians who share your commitment to live a holy life means you have someone to watch your back, so to speak. Often the people around us can see things coming that we're blind to. But if others are going to help us, we have to be open and transparent with them.

One of the Enemy's biggest lies is to convince us that "what I do is my own business, not anybody else's." That's simply not true. God called the church to be a community of the committed. We need spiritual soldiers who will go to war with us and fight with us in this battle.

As a pastor, when I see young people or families begin to draw back from the fellowship of the church I get very concerned. It means they're out there on their own in the world, and that's a very vulnerable position to be in. I love Ecclesiastes 4:9–10: "Two are better than one, because they have a good reward for their labor. For if they fall, one will lift up his companion. But woe to him who is alone when he falls, for he has no one to help him up."

There is power and strength in numbers. If the best decision you can make is to live a godly life, then the second-best decision you can make is to live a godly life in close connection with other people who share your commitment.

Self-reliance is not only stupid, it's sinful. Ask God to give you some people who know and love you and will call you on the carpet spiritually if necessary.

I have some people like that in my life. One of my longtime friends, Dr. O. S. Hawkins, and I made commitments together as young men to be morally pure and to hold each other accountable. We both went into the ministry, and God has kept us in such close proximity that more than thirty years later we still get together and talk about what's happening on the inside. I can't begin to tell you the difference this accountability has made in my life.

The problem with us men is that most of us have nobody to talk to. If we had a struggle, we wouldn't know who to discuss it with. Often men are not good at relationships, but that doesn't lessen our need for accountability.

These principles will give you a solid strategy for making your heart a place where Christ is not only at home but on the throne. Guard your heart, because out of it your life story is being told.

NOTES

1. Steve Green, "Guard Your Heart" © 1999 by Birdsong Music (a division of the Sparrow Corp.) (ASCAP). All rights administered by the Sparrow Corp. Used by permission.

2. Arthur Paul Boers, "Learning the Ancient Rhythms of Prayer," *Christianity Today,* 8 January 2001, 40.

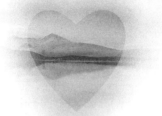

Chapter Four

GO WITH
GOD'S
FLOW

*T*here was a village in Europe whose cathedral contained beautiful, centuries-old stained glass windows. During World War II, air raids on the village threatened to destroy these treasures, so the townspeople took action. They dismantled the prized windows section by section and hid the sections in their homes for the duration of the war. Meanwhile, the cathedral stood stripped of its former glory until the windows were reassembled and put back in place after the war.

This cathedral and its dismantled windows are a good picture of the religion of Jesus' day. The Jewish authorities had stripped God's law of its glory and hidden its intended purpose, which was that of a "tutor to bring us to Christ, that we might be justified by faith" (Galatians 3:24).

The Pharisees and experts in the Jewish law did this by dismantling the Law of Moses like so many stained glass windows—taking it apart piece by piece and breaking it down into a set of external rules to be obeyed. In the process, they obscured the "big picture" of what God wanted from His people, which was and is a life of inner righteousness.

When Jesus came, He denounced this superficial legalism and called the people to true inward repentance and faith.

This was first-century Judaism, substituting hollow external performance for inward spiritual reality. But that could never happen to Christians in the twenty-first century, could it? Of course it could. We face the same temptation today to swap spiritual reality for empty religion. It's a problem we need to guard against, because the Christian faith always has been an issue of the heart. Jesus said that what matters most is what flows out from our hearts (see Mark 7:20–23).

The Lord chose one of the most important days on Israel's religious calendar to underscore the importance of this truth. On the climactic day of the Feast of Tabernacles, Jesus stood and cried out, "If anyone thirsts, let him come to Me and drink. He who believes in Me, as the Scripture has said, out of his heart will flow rivers of living water" (John 7:37b–38).

A PROMISE OF SATISFYING, OVERFLOWING LIFE

Jesus knew exactly what He was doing when He picked this occasion to make His startling announcement. The apostle John described the setting as "the last day, that great day of the feast" (John 7:37a).

The Feast of Tabernacles was one of the great festivals on the Jewish calendar, commemorating Israel's wanderings in the wilderness on the way from Egypt to Canaan (see Leviticus 23:33–44). Tabernacles was said to be the most joyous of all the Jewish festivals because it also celebrated the ingathering of the fall harvest.

One ceremony that was added to the feast later was the daily ritual of going to the Pool of Siloam, filling a golden pitcher with water, then bringing it back and pouring the water into a basin beside the altar. As the priest brought the water, the people sang and rejoiced.

This was the moment Jesus chose to step forward and make the life-changing offer of living water. John then explained, "But this He spoke concerning the Spirit, whom those believing in Him would receive; for the Holy Spirit was not yet given, because Jesus was not yet glorified" (John 7:39).

Enough of the Dry Dust

It's foolish to settle for the dry dust of man-made religion when God has a flowing river of joy, peace, and power for us. This is the message Jesus delivered on that dramatic day. We can imagine the scene. Jesus was standing in the middle of Jerusalem, which would have been packed with people, because the Feast of Tabernacles drew worshipers from all over Israel. There was pomp and celebration. The Levitical choirs were singing, and the crowds were waving branches in worship.

But if we look closer, we realize that it was all a ritual. And when it was over, the people went away the same as they were when they came. They had a religion with form but no force, plenty of pomp but no power with God.

Jesus must have watched the priest pouring water from the golden pitcher into the basin until He couldn't hold back any longer. "If you are parched for spiritual reality, come to Me and be satisfied!"

His words created quite a stir, because people immediately began wondering if Jesus was the promised prophet or perhaps the Messiah (John 7:40–41). Even the officers who were sent from the Pharisees and scribes to arrest Jesus said, "No man ever spoke like this Man!" (vv. 45–46).

The crowd was buzzing with excitement, because the people had become so used to the dry dust of Pharasaic religion they forgot there was any other way. Jesus whetted their spiritual thirst for the abundance that God wants to give His people.

An Explosion of Spiritual Power

When the Holy Spirit fills you and works within you, your life will explode with power. Satan will be on the run. You'll begin to break habits that are binding you. Your prayer life will take off. You'll become a witness, not just because you're supposed to but out of the Spirit's overflow within you.

The Savior's promise concerned the coming of the Holy Spirit to indwell believers in the new work God was going to do, called the church. The initial fulfillment of this promise came on the Day of Pentecost (Acts 2), and since then each person who knows Jesus Christ as Savior receives the Holy Spirit in all of His fullness at the moment of conversion.

Jesus described a Spirit-indwelt person as someone out of whose heart and life "rivers of living water" would flow in rushing streams of joy, power, praise, and worship.

Now if you're like me, this raises a question that begs for an answer. All of us know people whose lives don't match this description. They're saved, but they're not flowing with living water. There is no evidence of Holy Spirit power in their lives. And if we're honest with ourselves, we would also have to admit that there are times when our own hearts are more like parched deserts than flowing rivers.

That's not what I want, and I don't believe you do either. I want my heart to be a channel through whom the Holy Spirit can flow freely. There is something exciting and invigorating about a person like that. Thirsty people are attracted to someone who is living out of the overflow of an inner life energized by the Spirit of God.

How can we become people in whom and through whom the Holy Spirit flows like a mighty, rushing river? John 7 has some valuable answers in these power-packed verses.

MEETING JESUS AT THE WELL

We are made with an unquenchable thirst to know God—a thirst that will never be satisfied by anything or anyone but Him.

This is the universal human need Jesus was appealing to when He said, "If anyone thirsts, let him come to Me and drink" (John 7:37). He knew the people around Him were desperately thirsty for spiritual reality, even if they didn't know where to find it. So Jesus said in no uncertain terms, "I am the source of the water that will quench your thirst forever."

Satisfying Your Deepest Thirst

If we believe that God alone is the answer to the thirst in our souls, we can't afford to let anything come between us and the living water Jesus offers.

Earlier in His ministry, Jesus met a woman whose life is a vivid illustration of this truth. The Lord met this weary, wounded woman as He and His disciples passed through Samaria and she came to draw water from Jacob's well (John 4:1–7).

Jesus was resting by the well while the disciples went into the city to buy food. In the heat of the day, this woman came to get water.

She had a lot going against her. Being a Samaritan made her an outcast in the eyes of orthodox Jews, because Samaritans were people of mixed Jewish-Gentile descent and were considered half-breeds.

Not only that, but we learn that this woman was living a loose life that included five ex-husbands and a man she was living with at the time. She was a reject even among her own despised people, judging by two details in the text.

First, she came to the well alone, which most women wouldn't do because it wasn't safe. Second, she came at noon (vv. 6–7) when the sun was hot, instead of in the cool of the morning when women usually went to draw water. Evidently, none of the other women in her town wanted to be seen with this woman.

Sin had chewed her up and spit her out. But Jesus came that day to break through the pain and flood the desert of her heart with living water. As the woman pulled up her water pitcher, Jesus said, to her surprise, "Give Me a drink" (John 4:7).

That request began a conversation in which Jesus answered her surprise by saying, "If you knew the gift of God, and who it is who says to you, 'Give Me a drink,' you would have asked Him, and He would have given you living water" (v. 10).

The woman's response was skeptical, even a bit cynical (vv. 11–12). But that didn't deter Jesus. He replied with the same incredible offer He made later at the Feast of Tabernacles. "Whoever drinks of this water will thirst again, but whoever drinks of the water that I shall give him will never thirst. But the water that I shall give him will become in him a fountain of water springing up into everlasting life" (vv. 13b–14).

That got her attention! "Sir, give me this water" (v. 15). Jesus revealed this woman's desperate spiritual need to her, then revealed Himself and led her to the living water of eternal life. Before it was over she even became a missionary to the people of her town.

Power to Break Through the Barriers

The woman of Samaria had tried pleasure and multiple relationships, which left her heart dry and thirsty for something real. But when she drank the living water that Jesus offered her, she was changed forever. Her life became an overflowing stream that swept away the racial, religious, and relational barriers that had kept her shut up to sin.

There is no barrier to the power of Jesus Christ to change a life! He can provide the power to overcome anything that is keeping us from experiencing His fullness. To become a Christian is to drink of Jesus Christ, to take Him into your innermost being. By the greatest miracle of all, Jesus Christ enters your heart by His Spirit and begins to live His life through you.

Is it possible that the longing in your soul for God and for spiritual reality has never been met? If you're thirsty, accept the invitation of Jesus Christ to drink deeply of His grace and be satisfied!

Whatever you do, don't settle for any substitute—whether it's religion, pleasure, or things. Realize that neither your mate nor your money can satisfy the deepest need of your heart. Jesus' call is for you! Notice that there are no exceptions to His offer. "If anyone thirsts . . . He who believes in Me" (John 7:37–38). If you're thirsty for spiritual reality, come to Jesus and find real satisfaction.

THE OVERFLOWING POWER OF CHRIST WITHIN US

When we believe in Jesus Christ, the flow from within us through the Holy Spirit will be like "*rivers* of living water" (italics added). Not a spurt, a stream, or a trickle but a powerful flow of the Spirit of God.

An Unstoppable Force

I'm convinced that too many Christians have never fully understood the power resident within them in the Person of the Holy Spirit. His power is meant to be an unstoppable force flowing out of our lives.

I have a new appreciation for the power of flowing

water after hearing about the problems that a new home-owner in a fast-growing city near us had recently. There are areas in this particular city where the residential water pressure is three times the normal rate in anticipation of future growth. This young woman bought a home in one of these developments, which requires a special valve to modulate the water pressure. But her home's pressure valve malfunctioned, causing water damage that required more than $1,000 worth of repairs.

I'm grateful that we don't have to suppress the Holy Spirit's power in our lives. In fact, the Scripture cautions us, "Do not quench the Spirit" (1 Thessalonians 5:19).

A Dominating Power

When the Holy Spirit lives within us, it means that all the power of the Godhead lives within us. The Holy Spirit is not an inanimate force or an influence. He is the third Person of the Trinity, *God* the Holy Spirit.

Some Christians get nervous when the subject turns to the Holy Spirit and His limitless power. It sounds a little risky to talk about letting the Spirit flow freely in us, as if it might lead to some of the far-out demonstrations we've heard about in which people do strange things.

But don't allow the misguided teachings of some to keep you from knowing the joy and the power of the Spirit-filled life. The command of Ephesians 5:18 is for every believer. "Do not be drunk with wine, in which is dissipation; but be filled with the Spirit."

The analogy with wine teaches us that to be filled with the Spirit of God is to be under His control. Whatever controls you dominates your thinking and dictates your actions. When the power of the Holy Spirit is released in your life, you begin to act, think, talk, and live under His direction.

If you want to know overflowing power, don't let anything block the Spirit's work in your heart. Go with God's flow.

How do we get this river of life flowing in our hearts? Paul said, "As you therefore have received Christ Jesus the Lord, so walk in Him" (Colossians 2:6). In other words, we are filled with the Spirit the same way we are saved—by faith. Just as you trusted in Christ for salvation, so now ask and believe Him for the Spirit's filling in your heart on a day-by-day and moment-by-moment basis.

Jesus spoke of the importance of faith when He said, "He who believes in Me . . . out of his heart will flow rivers of living water" (John 7:38).

How do you know when you are developing a genuine thirst for God? Let me ask you a few questions. Do you have a passion for spiritual growth, a burning desire to know Christ? Do you get up in the morning thinking about your relationship with Christ and how you can please Him? Do you live in the awareness of the Holy Spirit's presence throughout the day, asking Him to guide, use, and bless you? This is what Jesus called abiding in Him (see John 15:4–5).

When we fall deeply in love with Jesus Christ . . . when our hearts beat with His . . . when we long to know and fellowship with Him . . . that's when the Spirit of God takes notice, because His purpose is to glorify Christ. When the Holy Spirit sees a believer with this kind of spiritual thirst, He says, "That's what I want. Let's get together."

The Christian life is intended to be a mighty flowing river. A Christian in bondage, with his or her life dammed up by sin or Satan, is a contradiction in terms because the Holy Spirit wants to sweep away every barrier that blocks His fullness within us.

THE OVERFLOWING POWER OF CHRIST TO OTHERS

It's in the nature of a river that the water keeps flowing. The opposite of a mighty river constantly on the move is a stagnant pond. That's why Jesus chose the word picture of a river to describe His fullness in our lives.

Filled to Overflowing

God wants the Holy Spirit to flow out of our hearts, not only for our blessing but so that we might be channels of blessing to others.

In Acts 1:8 Jesus said, "You shall receive power when the Holy Spirit has come upon you; and you shall be witnesses to Me in Jerusalem, and in all of Judea and Samaria, and to the end of the earth." Jesus spoke these words just days before the Holy Spirit came to indwell the church at Pentecost. Those early believers, filled with the Spirit, spilled out from Jerusalem like a flood that engulfed the whole world.

Our faith is not for our private enjoyment. The Holy Spirit wants to fill us to overflowing so that our lives will spill over and pour the refreshing water of life into parched and barren human hearts all over our world.

When you go with God's flow and begin living in the power of the Spirit, don't be surprised if others start getting splashed. People are going to come to you and ask, "What do you have that I don't have, and how can I get it?"

Sometimes we wonder, "Why has God put me in this job?" "What am I doing at this school?" "Why did God lead my family into this neighborhood where everyone seems to be a pagan?"

The answer is the same in each case. God has put you in that desert place so that rivers of living water might flow out from you to dying people who desperately need Jesus Christ.

Being a Difference-Maker

Do you want to make an eternal impact for Christ? Go with the flow of God's Spirit. You'll stop being a spectator of the action and start being a participator in the action. You'll be a difference-maker, not just a space-taker.

One man prayed, "Lord, make my life a fork in the road." He wanted to be so effective for Christ that when people met him, they were compelled to choose for or against Christ.

A friend of mine was on a tour of Israel several years ago when he had an opportunity to witness to one of the Arab guides in his group. This guide was interested in the gospel, and as my friend talked with him about his need of Christ, the man said, "Why hasn't anyone told me this before?" He had guided many Christians around Israel, but apparently no one had discussed the good news of Christ with him.

My friend began to apologize to his guide that no other believers had told him about Christ. Then the man said something very interesting. "Oh, I understand. It's the sin of the desert."

"What's the sin of the desert?" my friend asked.

The guide replied, "The sin of the desert is when a man knows where there is water but doesn't tell others." I never want to be guilty of that sin.

Let's not be like Jesus' disciples on the day He met the Samaritan woman at the well. The Bible tells us the disciples went into town that day to buy food. They spent the morning shopping, and they didn't bring anybody back with them from town to meet Jesus.

But when that sinful woman drank from the water of eternal life that Jesus offered, her life began overflowing immediately. She ran back into town to tell other thirsty people where they could find living water. Go with the flow of the Spirit of God, and you'll make the same kind of difference.

Chapter Five

THE CURE
FOR A
DISEASED HEART

*T*he U.S. government's intelligence community was sent reeling early in 2001 when veteran FBI agent Robert Hanssen was arrested and charged with spying for Russia. Hanssen's years of counterintelligence work had given him access to a wide range of classified information about U.S. counterintelligence operations. He was arrested after FBI agents observed him leaving a package of classified documents at a Virginia park for pickup by Russian agents.

The story also sent shock waves among those who thought they knew Robert Hanssen. One neighbor said of the accused spy's family, "They go to church every Sunday—if that means anything—loading all six kids into the van."

The case of Robert Hanssen illustrates how hard it is for us to know what is in a person's heart. We can fool ourselves and other people about the true condition of our hearts, but we cannot escape the penetrating gaze of God.

His Word says that God has looked directly into the

depths of the human heart, and the news is not good. All of us in our natural condition are separated from God and without hope because our hearts are corrupted by the disease of sin.

Paul summarized mankind's spiritual dilemma in two classic statements from his letter to the Romans. "For all have sinned and fall short of the glory of God" (3:23). "For the wages of sin is death" (6:23).

The prophet Jeremiah used the heart as the center of a person's being to describe the problem: "The heart is deceitful above all things, and desperately wicked; who can know it?" (17:9). David declared, "Behold, I was brought forth in iniquity" (Psalm 51:5).

Since we're discussing foundational issues related to the heart, we need to talk about why people are born with diseased hearts, spiritually speaking, and what can be done about it. In other words, how bad off is the human race in the eyes of God, and what does it take to solve the problem?

You may be thinking that sin and salvation are basic, ABC-type doctrines that most Christians already know and believe, and you're probably right. If you didn't believe what the Bible teaches about human sin and our need for salvation, you most likely would not be reading this book.

But even if this matter is clear in your own mind and heart, the chances are good that it's not at all clear to your neighbor, the person next to you at work, or even all of your family members. I'd be willing to say that the majority of the people on this planet don't have a clear sense of what their responsibility before God is, or what they should do about it. That's why I want to review what the Bible says about the diseased human heart and the cure that God has provided in Jesus Christ. People are incredibly confused about the nature of sin and what it takes to get to heaven. We need to know what we believe for our own well-being and to help point the people around us to Christ.

THE HEART'S SPIRITUALLY FATAL DISEASE

Jeremiah said the human heart is deceitful and wicked. That's about as bad as it gets.

Theologians often use the term *depravity* to describe a lost person's condition. Depravity doesn't mean we're all as bad as we can be. It means we're all as bad *off* as we can be. There is nothing good within us to commend us to God or cause Him to accept us. That's exactly what Jeremiah was saying. Our heart disease is total, and ultimately fatal, apart from the grace of God.

Dabbling in the Spiritual

Now don't misunderstand. The fact that human beings have depraved hearts and are cut off from God does not necessarily mean they have no interest in spiritual things. Just the opposite may be true.

Ask a thousand people on the street if they want to go to heaven when they die, and most will probably say, "Of course." A good number might also answer in the affirmative if asked whether they feel they're going to make it to heaven. A lot of people are interested in the afterlife and the spiritual dimension of this life.

One of the ironies of our post-Christian age is a surge of interest in spiritual matters. Go to a secular bookstore and look at the sections labeled "Religion" or "Inspirational" or something similar.

A large chain bookstore in Dallas has an impressive amount of shelf space devoted to inspirational books. You can get a Bible in several versions, commentaries and other Bible study aids, and some other solid Christian works. The problem is that in the same section you'll find books on every imaginable religion and form of false spirituality, including the occult. This particular bookstore even has a book attacking the Bible as a hoax—nothing but a compilation from other ancient works.

One reason for this proliferation of books is that people dabble in spirituality like someone in a cafeteria line. They want to try a little of this and a taste of that. Much of this interest is self-centered. It's safe to say that a good portion of those who are dabbling in various spiritualities and mystic philosophies are not interested in self-denial and spiritual discipline. They're looking for something to meet their personal needs, improve their relationships and personal performance, or make them feel better about themselves.

This self-interest isn't limited to the non-Christian world, either. New research data on Christian young people reveal that among their top reasons for going to church are to seek relationships and to have fun activities in a safe environment.

When asked to rank nineteen future goals in order of importance in their lives, these same young people ranked "having a close personal relationship with God" as eighth overall. "Being committed to the Christian faith" ranked *fourteenth* of the nineteen goals. The researchers said that the seven top future goals for this group of young Christians all related to having satisfying relationships or a comfortable way of life.

If those inside the church are confused about what constitutes true spiritual reality, we shouldn't be surprised that religion is confusing to the world.

So lost people may have an intense, though seriously misguided, interest in spiritual things. They may even say to Christians, as they often do, "What gives you the right to claim that all other religions are wrong and that Christians are the only ones going to heaven?"

The answer, of course, is that we don't make that claim. This is the clear teaching of Scripture. Jesus Himself declared, "I am the way, the truth, and the life. No one comes to the Father except through Me" (John 14:6).

Jesus taught the exclusiveness of the way of eternal life. "Broad is the way that leads to destruction, and there are many who go in by it. [But] narrow is the gate and difficult is the way which leads to life, and there are few who find it" (Matthew 7:13–14). The sobering reality is that more people are going to hell than going to heaven.

Trying to Fill the Void

Sin will doom a person for eternity unless the solution of salvation is applied. But sin also leaves a gaping void in the human heart that cries out to be filled. People whose hearts are diseased by sin try all kinds of substitutes to fill that void.

One woman said she was miserable and lost without Christ even though she did all the "right" things such as get a college education, get married, and have children, just the way her parents wanted her to do.

Many young people think, *If I can get my college degree and prepare myself for a good career, that will satisfy me. I'll be on my way up in life.* They get their education and enter the right career, but somehow it's not enough. So they decide that if they can find the right person, get married and settle down, they'll be content. But real fulfillment continues to escape them.

Then they conclude that they need children to round out their family and make their lives complete. So the children come along, but the deep void in their hearts is still there.

That must mean it's time to upgrade the house. When they first got married, these people had a house with a porch and a white picket fence, just like the happy families on the TV programs. But now they want a bigger house. Not a mansion, just something nice they can be proud of.

But when all of that fails to satisfy the longing in their hearts, these people decide what they really need to do is enjoy themselves more. So they start looking for a vacation house they can retreat to on the weekends. And after that, they start looking toward the future and open a retirement account.

Nothing seems to fill the void, though, and they're left wondering, *Why does everything I do eventually leave me empty? Why is everything so temporary?* They begin feeling restless and antsy, like having an itch that you can't scratch. But that aching void in their hearts just won't go away.

Refusing the Cure

I don't know anybody who enjoys pain so much he or she is unwilling to give it up. If you had a diseased heart and were living in severe pain, and there was a complete and lasting cure available, would you be interested?

The answer to that question seems pretty obvious at first glance. So why don't more unsaved people turn to Jesus Christ and receive His forgiveness and healing? Why would they avoid the cure of repentance and salvation when it's readily available—and free?

I think there are several practical reasons that people don't come to Christ. Some simply haven't yet got the message that there *is* a cure for the disease of sin. It's our job to get the word out to them (we'll talk more about evangelism in a later chapter).

Other people are really interested in the cure, but they misunderstand what it involves and requires of them. Let me give you an example. An unsaved person will look at a Christian friend or co-worker and think, *I wish I had what Bob has. He seems so happy, so at peace with himself and the world. I know he's religious, but he's not a freak. He seems to be for real. He has problems like everyone else, but he handles them so much better than I do.*

A lot of lost people genuinely admire the authentic Christians around them, and they secretly wish they could get it together like these believers. But they hang back because of some preconceived ideas about what it means to be a Christian. They misunderstand the nature of the cure.

For instance, an unsaved person may reason, "Yes, I really admire Bob, but I could never be like that. It's just not in my nature to be religious. I fail too many times. I could never live the life."

That's exactly what a professional athlete once told his team's chaplain. This ballplayer thought that being a Christian meant trying to clean up and reform his lifestyle, and he was enjoying the fleshly pleasures of fame and wealth. So he told the chaplain, "I know I need to become a Christian, but with all these things available to me I know I could never live the life."

You could argue that this athlete's problem wasn't a misunderstanding of what being a Christian involves but an unwillingness to turn from his sin. That's another major reason people avoid or refuse the cure for a diseased heart.

We need to remember that some people love their sin more than they hate the pain of an empty life. Jesus wept over Jerusalem and said, "How often I wanted to gather your children together, as a hen gathers her chicks under her wings, but you were not willing!" (Matthew 23:37).

People like this *do* understand what it costs to put their faith in Christ and follow Him, but they're not willing to take the risk and pay the price. They know they're stuck in a rut. But although ruts may not be very much fun, they're at least predictable and don't demand much effort.

Whatever people's reasons for refusing the cure, their problem is the same: heart disease. A radical cure is needed, and that's what happens when a lost person turns to Christ and is saved.

THE RADICAL CURE OF SALVATION

We dare not compromise on the message of the gospel to make it more attractive to unbelievers.

I've been using words like "fatal disease" and "radical cure" to describe the problem of sin and the remedy of salvation. If we allow ourselves to get fuzzy on the Bible's teaching that sin is eternally fatal and incurable apart from Christ, we'll wind up offering placebos to people who need a heart transplant.

Salvation doesn't come about by reformation or behavior modification. It is an experience that is so radical it is like getting a brand-new heart.

A Transforming *Change of Heart*

No one can come to Jesus Christ and remain in a sinful lifestyle, because salvation results in a total transformation of a person's life. Jesus said that to believe in Him was to pass "from death into life" (John 5:24; also 1 John 3:14).

Paul gave us a classic statement of this transforming life change when he wrote, "If anyone is in Christ, he is a new creation; old things have passed away; behold, all things have become new" (2 Corinthians 5:17).

This new creation involves a heart change. Speaking through the prophet Ezekiel, God told the rebellious people of Israel, "I will give you a new heart and put a new spirit within you; I will take the heart of stone out of your flesh and give you a heart of flesh" (Ezekiel 36:26).

The message of salvation is good news to people who are trying to chip away at their diseased, stony hearts in order to make themselves acceptable to God. The good news is that they can give up their useless and frustrating effort because God has a new heart waiting for them.

In order to have this life-changing experience, we must be willing to repent of our sins. Repentance means a change of mind and heart about ourselves, about our sin, and about Jesus Christ that leads to a change of direction.

One night Jesus sat down with a Pharisee named Nicodemus, a very wise rabbi and one of the most brilliant men of his time. Nicodemus came to Jesus seeking answers to issues of the heart. Jesus looked at this sophisticated, well-educated, and well-respected religious leader and said, "Most assuredly, I say to you, unless one is born again, he cannot see the kingdom of God" (John 3:3).

Nicodemus immediately thought Jesus was speaking of physical birth and asked how it was possible for a person to be born a second time. But Jesus was speaking of spiritual rebirth, a radically new concept to Nicodemus. Jesus saw his consternation and said again, "Do not marvel that I said to you, 'You must be born again'" (John 3:7).

Nicodemus had every reason to believe that as a Jew and a Pharisee and a leader in Israel, he had been born right the first time. Paul thought that of himself too, before He met Christ and found out that true righteousness comes through faith in Christ (see Philippians 3:3–9).

But Jesus told Nicodemus that nothing short of a rebirth by the Spirit of God would qualify a person for heaven. Salvation involves a complete change of life and heart . . . a miracle of transformation that only God can accomplish.

When we invite Jesus Christ into our lives, He gives us brand-new hearts. He doesn't patch us up or put Band-Aids on our souls to hide the fact that our hearts are desperately diseased and wicked.

If you have been a Christian for a number of years, chances are it has been a while since you sat back and thought about the radical spiritual surgery required to bring you from death to life and replace your diseased spiritual heart with a new one.

Every time I turn to God's Word, I realize again that I can't afford to pull any punches or be fuzzy in presenting the gospel. If I am not crystal clear on the issue, unsaved people won't get the message about their desperate condition and the life-transforming change they need to experience.

Aren't you glad God doesn't demand that we try to

clean up our lives before we can come to Him? We can't change ourselves by wishing or trying any more than a caterpillar can become a butterfly simply by wishing it to happen. A caterpillar becomes a butterfly by yielding itself to the radical process of metamorphosis.

Salvation demands a total change of heart, initiated by God through His grace and love. The Bible says, "God demonstrates His own love toward us, in that while we were still sinners, Christ died for us" (Romans 5:8).

A Thorough *Cleansing from Sin*

Salvation is also a cleansing experience because it deals with the problem of guilt we all feel for the wrong things we've done and the right things we've left undone. In Ezekiel 36:25, God said through the prophet, "I will sprinkle clean water on you, and you shall be clean; I will cleanse you from all your filthiness and from all your idols."

This prophecy looked forward to the new covenant of salvation and cleansing that was instituted at the death and resurrection of Jesus Christ. For rebellious Israel, this blessing will be realized when God gathers His scattered people together. But we as believers today already enjoy the blessings of redemption. That's why Jesus said at the Last Supper, "This cup is the new covenant in My blood, which is shed for you" (Luke 22:20).

Listen to this wonderful invitation to cleansing from the Lord. "'Come now, and let us reason together,' says the Lord. 'Though your sins are like scarlet, they shall be as white as snow; though they are red like crimson, they shall be as wool'" (Isaiah 1:18). In salvation God not only gives us a new heart, but He also cleanses us of every stain and blot and blemish left behind by our old hearts.

The cleansing of salvation also has a present aspect to it, explained by the apostle John in a verse I hope you have memorized and you apply regularly. "If we confess our sins, He is faithful and just to forgive us our sins and to cleanse us from all unrighteousness" (1 John 1:9).

When we fail as Christians and our hearts are stained by the guilt of sin, we can come to the Savior in confession and repentance and be cleansed. This isn't salvation itself but the everyday cleansing from sin that the blood of Jesus Christ makes possible for us. The old hymn says it well: "His blood can wash away each stain."

The Ongoing Presence of Christ

God has committed Himself to us for eternity! He'll never leave us or give up on us. The reason we can obey Christ and grow in Him as Christians is that God is at work in us "both to will and to do for His good pleasure" (Philippians 2:13).

First John 1:9 is one example of the fact that salvation is an ongoing experience. It's not something that happens today and is over and forgotten tomorrow. God also spoke to our need for ongoing grace in Ezekiel 36:27: "I will put My Spirit within you and cause you to walk in My statutes, and you will keep My judgments and do them."

God isn't interested in providing "fire insurance" salvation that keeps us out of hell but does nothing in or through us today. In the Bible, to "walk" in obedience to God is a reference to our way of life. Another name for salvation is eternal life, because this cure is good for eternity!

Paul told the Philippians, "Work out your own salvation with fear and trembling" (2:12). The context here is the believer's obedience to Christ as a way of life. Some people pull back from committing their lives to Christ because they're afraid they can't live the life.

The truth is, they're right! No one has ever lived the Christian life successfully except Jesus Christ Himself. That's why the Christian life is a matter of "Christ in you"

(Colossians 1:27). At salvation, Christ comes to live His life in and through us by the power of the Holy Spirit.

Jesus Christ paid the eternal price for sin so that God could gather to Himself a people for eternity—the saved of all the ages.

There's nothing temporary about salvation. The disease of sin has so radically damaged the human heart that nothing less than a new heart will fix the problem. Jesus Christ will give everyone who comes to Him a brand-new heart.

Chapter Six

RESTORING YOUR SPIRITUAL PASSION

I admire people who do what they do with real passion, giving it everything they've got. It seems to me it's not worth taking on a task unless you're going to do it with gusto and commitment. We often say of people like this that they really put their hearts into what they're doing. That's an accurate statement biblically, which is why I want us to consider passion as another issue of the heart.

Passion comes in many varieties. The sports world is filled with illustrations of people who lived with a burning desire to be the best and use every ounce of their ability. One such person is Bart Starr, the great quarterback of the Green Bay Packers in their heyday of the sixties and seventies. Starr said this about his coach, the late Vince Lombardi:

> I wasn't mentally tough before I met Coach Lombardi. I
> hadn't reached the point where I refused to accept second
> best. I was too nice at times. . . . To win, you have to have a
> certain amount of mental toughness. Coach Lombardi gave

me that. He taught me that you must have a flaming desire to win. It's got to dominate all your waking hours. It can't ever wane. It's got to glow in you all of the time.[1]

I could give you many more examples like these. It's fun to meet people who perform their ministry or their craft with passion. But we also have to face the fact that it is possible for the flame of our spiritual passion to dim and go out.

A DOUSED FLAME OF SPIRITUAL PASSION

I'm confident that, like me, you've known times when you were totally drained, exhausted, out of gas. This loss is so common in our fast-paced world that it has a name: burnout.

Burnout can be defined as a state of mental, physical, emotional, or spiritual fatigue. It can be brought on by good things, such as devotion to a worthy cause or ministry. In fact, Christians are very prone to burnout, because they are committed to what they're doing and want to serve the Lord.

But whatever the cause, we are seeing an epidemic of people who have lost their passion for life. They have burned out, bottomed out, and, in some cases, dropped out. Some have walked out on their families or abdicated other responsibilities. A number of burned-out pastors have chosen to leave their churches. A lot of people today have been set up for burnout, which leads to a loss of passion, by the insane pace of modern life. Maybe you feel like you're running on empty right now, or that you're in a rat race and the rats are winning. If so, my hope is that the biblical principles in this chapter will help refresh and renew your heart and restore your spiritual passion.

People reveal the symptoms of burnout in their conversations. Think about how often you have heard someone say, "I'm overcommitted," "I've got to find some time for myself," "My schedule is out of control right now," or, "I'm tired of being tired all the time."

A loss of passion in life can be the result of physical exhaustion, but more often than not it comes from a tired spirit. Too many people are bored with their lives. Everything has become bland, boring, and routine. This sense of boredom and sameness can also invade Christians' church involvement and their service for the Lord.

The problem is not that the Christian life is boring. Far from it! But we can allow frustration with ourselves, disappointment with others, or unfulfilled expectations to get the best of us, and before we know it we have grown weary. Paul even warned against this. He urged, "Let us not grow weary while doing good" (Galatians 6:9).

Spiritual, emotional, and physical weariness is part of our imperfect human condition. So let's admit that even for followers of Jesus Christ, a loss of spiritual passion is not only possible but even probable at some point along the way.

REKINDLING THE FLAME OF SPIRITUAL PASSION

The good news is that a loss of passion can be reversed. We don't have to remain stuck in our routine or rut. To learn how we can restore our spiritual passion, I want us to walk with two discouraged, empty, and passionless disciples on their way back home after what they thought was the biggest letdown of their lives.

The story is the familiar account of the two disciples on the road to Emmaus (Luke 24:13–53). Let me set the stage so we can concentrate on several key verses that show us how spiritual passion can be restored.

The irony of these disciples' discouragement is that it came on the day of Jesus' resurrection (see Luke 24:1–12). They were deeply disappointed and crushed in spirit because their greatest fears had come to pass. Jesus of Nazareth had been crucified and buried in a borrowed tomb in Jerusalem. Their dreams were deflated. Jesus had not proved to be the hoped-for Messiah after all (vv. 19–21).

Their dismay is really amazing because they had heard the astonishing news that Jesus' tomb was empty (vv. 22–24), but they refused to believe it. The flame of these disciples' passion had definitely been doused as they walked along the road from Jerusalem to their home in Emmaus, about seven miles to the northwest.

Don't Let Disappointments Deflate You

One thing that can lead to the loss of spiritual passion is disappointment over unfulfilled expectations. That was the case with the Emmaus disciples. Somewhere on their journey, the risen Christ joined them, although they didn't recognize Him (Luke 24:15–16)—unbelief had closed their eyes to the fact that it was Jesus Himself. He engaged them in a conversation that climaxed with a dramatic revelation of Himself.

But notice that the first thing Jesus did was probe the reason for their obvious sadness and loss of zeal. I'll summarize verses 17–27. Jesus asked these disciples, "What have you been talking about, and why do you look so sad?"

That's all it took. The men were aghast that this stranger didn't seem to know all that had just happened in Jerusalem, and they proceeded to explain their problem. "We're discouraged because Jesus of Nazareth, the One we believed was the Messiah, the One we hoped would deliver us from the tyranny of Rome, was betrayed by our own religious leaders and executed by the Romans. Now even His body is missing."

They were clearly disappointed, but don't stop there, because Jesus was *not* the reason for their disappointment. He never disappoints anyone!

It's one thing to be deflated and defeated because some-one let you down or because you let yourself down. But if you are struggling with the loss of spiritual passion, be assured that Jesus is not the cause. He never fails!

The disciples on the Emmaus road had put their hopes in the right place but had let unbelief cloud their minds and hearts. Unbelief is sin, which is why Jesus addressed them so sharply:

> "O foolish ones, and slow of heart to believe in all that the prophets have spoken! Ought not the Christ to have suf-fered these things and to enter into His glory?" And begin-ning at Moses and all the Prophets, He expounded to them in all the Scriptures the things concerning Himself. (Luke 24:25–27)

Imagine these two flamed-out followers of Christ, walking along a dark road. They had lost the passion that makes life sizzle and that gives us the spiritual energy to serve Christ with energy, effectiveness, and deep-seated joy.

Confidence in Christ is never misplaced. Sadly, we can't say the same about the hopes and expectations we place in other people. If you are depending on anyone but Christ to keep you joyful and motivated, you're in a canoe headed for a waterfall!

Make sure you keep your eyes firmly fixed on Jesus so you won't be devastated by life's inevitable disappoint-ments.

Putting the Color Back in Life

Not all discouraged, defeated, and passionless disciples drop out on life. Many just settle for less, going through the motions of Christian worship and service even though their faith has lost its color.

I can remember when our family got its first television in 1954. It was a beautiful Philco brand, with a black-and-white picture. That was the only kind of television we knew about. I would sit for hours in front of that television, watching the *Mickey Mouse Club, Howdy Doody, The Pinky Lee Show*—all the greats and near-greats of the fifties. I was so happy with that wonderful television.

But then some of my friends in the neighborhood got color television. I couldn't believe what those same programs looked like in color. Suddenly my old black-and-white television wasn't so magical. I started spending more time over at my friends' houses, watching those programs in vivid color.

Many Christians today remind me of black-and-white television. There is no color or vividness to their lives. There's not the full force and energy of life that Christ intends us to have.

RESTORING SPIRITUAL PASSION: THE PRINCIPLE OF REVELATION

We don't know if the disciples on the Emmaus road were getting ready to drop out on the faith and go home. But it seems pretty evident that the spiritual color had gone out of their lives. Their faces told the story. Jesus could tell they were sad just by looking at them. They thought their dream was dead and buried in a tomb outside Jerusalem.

But Jesus came alongside them that night to restore their faith and their spiritual passion, just as He comes today to restore the passion and color of life for you and me.

How did He do this for the Emmaus disciples? Let me suggest four ways that Jesus ministered to these men. We can state them in the form of four principles that can help us rekindle our spiritual passion.

When burnout and loss of spiritual passion threaten to take us down, we need a fresh *revelation* of who Jesus is.

The trouble with the Emmaus disciples is that they were going by what they had heard and what they thought. They had the right idea about Jesus, that He was Israel's Messiah, but they abandoned that hope when they left Jerusalem. They figured it was a case of mistaken identity and misplaced hope.

Find Out Who Jesus Really Is

When our spiritual passion is at low ebb, it's time to be reminded of who God is and the way He works. Here's what I mean. When life's hurts or the actions of other people knock us down and rob us of our spiritual vigor, we usually want God to come in a blaze of power and glory and deliver us. God may reveal Himself in that way—or He may have other purposes in mind for us.

For instance, we know from Scripture that God uses hard times to teach us contentment (Philippians 4:11–12). He uses suffering to teach us that His grace is sufficient (2 Corinthians 12:7–10) and to help us know Him better (Philippians 3:10). There's a very important principle of revelation in these passages. Read them and you'll see that, in each case, Paul's reaction was basically the same: "Lord, if this is what You want for me, if it will help me know You better and experience Your power, bring it on. I'm well content with poverty and weakness and suffering!" This man was fired up and ready to take on the world for Christ.

In other words, Paul's spiritual passion wasn't based on a wallet full of money and a life free of pain and problems. It was based on revelation, the knowledge of who Jesus is and what He wants to do through His people.

Get Your Information Firsthand

Too many of us live secondhand Christian lives. We're content to know what the preacher says about God, or what the latest best-selling author has discovered. The problem of Luke 24 is our problem today. These disciples were operating on hearsay, on secondhand information about the events of that first Easter Sunday.

There is no substitute for firsthand knowledge of God. He wants us to know and experience the same truths Paul discovered. That's why these things are in God's Word. Jesus doesn't literally walk along the road with you and me, but He reveals Himself and speaks to us in His Word.

The Emmaus disciples got an eye-opening revelation from Scripture (Luke 24:27), a full-length course in Old Testament delivered by Jesus Himself. He began at Genesis 1:1 and showed how every part of the Bible speaks of Him.

I meet with a lot of people who are struggling with life. Perhaps their marriages or their children have disappointed them, or their careers have left them unfulfilled. What a privilege it is to open the Scriptures and introduce people to the living Christ, because that's when life begins to make sense.

"Faith comes by hearing, and hearing by the word of God" (Romans 10:17). It is in the Word of God that we meet the risen Christ, not the Christ of our or someone else's imagination.

We must encounter the living Lord for ourselves. How about you? Have you walked with Him and heard His voice today as you met Him in the Word? The first step in restoring your spiritual passion is to know the reality of Jesus Christ by the revelation of Scripture.

RESTORING SPIRITUAL PASSION: THE PRINCIPLE OF RELATIONSHIPS

Even though the Emmaus disciples lived a long distance from Jerusalem for that day, they were clearly part of the body of disciples who followed Jesus. Their lives illustrate the principle of *relationships*.

Become Part of the Company

If you want to recapture your spiritual passion, one of the most important things you can do is to develop relationships with other believers who will spark your faith and encourage you in the way.

The Emmaus disciples identified themselves as in the "company" of those who believed in Jesus (Luke 24:22). They were even with the apostles on Resurrection Day because "certain of those who were with *us* went to the tomb" (v. 24, italics added). Those who went to the tomb were Peter and John.

So these men were in close relationship with the larger body of believers in Jerusalem. They also identified with each other when they said, "Did not *our* heart burn within *us* while He talked with *us* on the road, and while He opened the Scriptures to *us?*" (v. 32, italics added).

These two disciples had a brief lapse of faith, and it needed to be dealt with. But they were not living in spiritual isolation. As soon as they realized that they had seen the risen Lord, they headed straight back to Jerusalem to the apostles, and they were there when Jesus appeared again (vv. 33–36).

Join with Other People

Being in vital spiritual relationship with other Christians has its risks and rewards . . . and it's the only way to live. All kinds of people walk in and out of our lives. Some people drain us of our spiritual and emotional energy, leaving us feeling empty. Other people drive us. They push and prod us to keep doing more, to work harder. They leave us feeling spent and exhausted.

But praise the Lord for those people who develop us. These are the special men and women in our lives who encourage and challenge us to be at our best for the Lord and equip us for the task. All of us need people like this around us.

God did not design you to live an independent Christian life, separated from other believers. That's why He placed you in the body of Christ, the "fellowship of the flaming heart," which is the church of Jesus Christ. Find a group of Christians with hearts aflame for Christ and ablaze with spiritual passion, and it will ignite you as well.

Burn Together or Burn Out

Believers are like logs on a fire. Take a log off the fire and put it on the hearth by itself, and it will flicker and burn out. But put those logs together, and you've got a roaring fire. We men in particular tend to be like individual logs trying to burn alone. A lot of men have acquaintances, but not many have the kind of friends and mentors who know them well enough and are close enough to challenge them to growth in Christ.

But the book of Hebrews urges all of us to stir one another up for the purpose of good works and not to forsake our assembling together (see Hebrews 10:24–25). The Scripture also teaches, "As iron sharpens iron, so a man sharpens the countenance of his friend" (Proverbs 27:17). The principle works for women too.

As a good illustration of this principle, the latter verses of Luke 24 record the remarkable conclusion of the Emmaus disciples' story. When they returned to the fellowship of believers, they ended up being renewed in their joy. We have every reason to believe they were also among the disciples who experienced the Holy Spirit's coming at Pentecost and became passionate witnesses for Christ.

RESTORING SPIRITUAL PASSION: THE PRINCIPLE OF RESURRECTION

If you want to restore your spiritual passion, you can't do any better than to experience *resurrection*. The problem with the disciples Jesus met on the way to Emmaus was that they were living on the wrong side of the Resurrection. They were living back in the seeming defeat of the Cross.

Be Empowered by Christ's Life

Many Christians who have been to the Cross for pardon have not been to the empty tomb for power. Paul made an important statement in Romans 5:10: "If when we were enemies we were reconciled to God through the death of His Son, much more, having been reconciled, we shall be saved by His life."

We are saved from the judgment of God by Christ's death on the cross. We're forgiven because Christ paid the price for our sins on the cross. But we are also saved by His life. That is, we are saved by the power of the resurrected Christ, who is resident within us through the Holy Spirit. That's why Paul could summarize the Christian life as "Christ in you, the hope of glory" (Colossians 1:27).

The disciples we're reading about in Luke 24 pled with Jesus to stay with them that night when they reached Emmaus. It was in their home, as He blessed and broke bread and gave it to them, that Jesus was revealed as their resurrected Lord (vv. 28–31).

Later, these men told the other disciples that Jesus became known to them "in the breaking of bread" (v. 35). I like that because it tells me that resurrection power meets us right where we are, in the ordinary events of everyday life. Jesus and these disciples were simply having a meal together when that event was infused with resurrection glory.

There was no thunder or flashes of lightning when the resurrected Christ made His presence felt. The men didn't see angels or hear voices. But they knew beyond a doubt that Jesus was alive.

Come Close to the Flame

Because Jesus is alive, every day is Easter and every experience is an Easter experience, whether we're commuting to work, eating a meal, or sitting in church. God never intended for any of us to live the Christian life in our own strength. We are to be fueled by the fire of the Resurrection. Knowing that you have the power of Christ within you ought to do something to elevate your spiritual passion.

I wonder what would have happened if these disciples had been content merely to say good-bye to Jesus and turn away when He indicated He wanted to keep going (Luke 24:28). We don't know whether Jesus would have revealed Himself to them anyway. Probably not, because He wanted to make sure that they really wanted His fellowship before joining them for dinner. How badly do you want the resurrected Lord to sit at your table?

The disciples' invitation was insistent. Their hearts were already burning from Jesus' Bible teaching on the way, and they wanted more of the inner fire this stranger had ignited. If you want to restore your spiritual passion, you don't necessarily have to catch the next seminar or retreat. Just plug into resurrection power right there at your own table, in the everyday events of life.

The Bible says, "Draw near to God and He will draw near to you" (James 4:8). Come close to the flame of the living Christ, and your heart will burn with renewed passion.

RESTORING SPIRITUAL PASSION: THE PRINCIPLE OF REALIGNMENT

Whenever our passion for the things of Christ begins to wane, it's time to check our spiritual alignment. Maybe we're being pulled off course by discouragement, sin, or setbacks, the way a car out of alignment often pulls to one side or the other. It's worth noting that when the Emmaus disciples went back to Jerusalem that night, they were returning to the scene of their previous defeat and failure.

Besides the fact that they had astonishing news to tell, the disciples' return was sort of an admission to themselves that they had been wrong and needed to make things right. This is the principle of spiritual restoration that I call *realignment*.

Get Back into the Action

Before they met Jesus, these two men were on the road to nowhere, heading back home to defeat and oblivion. But now their hearts were inflamed with the fire of Christ, and they wanted to get realigned with Jesus' program. So they immediately returned to Jerusalem to be at the center of the action.

Their commitment was amply rewarded when Jesus appeared again and taught the group of disciples gathered together (Luke 24:45). The Emmaus followers even got to witness Jesus' ascension (vv. 50–51), after which they "returned to Jerusalem with great joy, and were continually in the temple praising and blessing God" (vv. 52–53).

What a great picture of renewed spiritual passion. These broken, burned-out, and wiped-out followers of Jesus Christ were now worshiping, praising, and joyously serving Him. And when Pentecost came, they became His witnesses in Jerusalem and ultimately to the world. They had a new mission in life.

If we want to get spiritually realigned and rejuvenated, we need to ask God to give us a new vision of His kingdom, the mission that's bigger than our own little world.

Someone has said that if Jesus Christ is still in His grave, then nothing matters. But if Jesus Christ is alive, then nothing *else* matters! What should get us up each day and stoke our passion for life is the opportunity to be a witness to the living reality of Jesus Christ in our lives.

Toss the Trinkets

Well-known author Calvin Miller tells the story of an old wooden dynamite box that he has among his collection of antiques. On top of that box in bold letters is a warning of danger, because the box was made to hold dynamite.

But Miller says that inside his antique dynamite box is nothing but a collection of nuts and bolts and other common paraphernalia. That's a description of too many Christians. We have been infused with the dynamite power of the resurrected Christ, yet too often our lives are filled with the rusted trinkets of the world instead of exploding with spiritual energy.

If your spiritual passion is at a low ebb right now, go before God on your knees with His open Word before you, and stay there until God reignites the flame. Then share the glow with other believers who need rekindling too. And if your spiritual passion is aflame right now, get on your knees and ask God to help you keep the flame lit.

NOTE

1. Jerry Kramer, ed. *Lombardi: Winning Is the Only Thing* (New York: Pocket Books, 1970), 86.

Chapter Seven

GIVING UP
WITHOUT
GIVING IN

In the days of the great Western cattle ranches, cattle-men had an interesting way of breaking wild horses. An unbroken stallion would be harnessed to a little burro, and the two of them would be let loose out onto the range.

At first the stallion would kick and buck and drag the burro around like a sack of wheat. The two might be gone for days, but eventually they would return with the burro leading the now-docile horse. That wild stallion had exhausted itself trying to break free of the burro, but it had given up the fight, and its power was now harnessed, ready to serve the rancher.

That's exactly what it means to give up without giving in. Jesus Christ calls us to yield control of our lives to Him, so that we might be useful to Him by becoming all that He wants us to be.

Admittedly, this is not always easy to do, because most of us like the feeling of being in control. Besides, giving in sounds like giving up, as if we're quitting. Even though that's not the case, of all the heart issues we will discuss this may be the most difficult of all to put into practice. We're afraid that if we give up control, our lives are somehow going to spin out of their orbits. So we try to guide our own destinies and call the shots.

But it's not until we yield control that the Lord Jesus Christ can take His rightful place of lordship in our hearts. The Lord does not simply want a place in our lives, or even priority. He demands *pre-eminence*. It has been said many times: If Jesus Christ is not Lord of all, He is not Lord at all. So the call is to give ourselves unconditionally and unreservedly to the leadership of the Holy Spirit and the lordship of Jesus Christ.

To get at the heart of this issue, I want to examine a passage of Scripture that explodes with spiritual power. It's a prayer in which the apostle Paul bowed in humility and submission before God, praying that His people might be filled with all of His fullness so our lives will radiate His glory.

This dynamic prayer is found in Ephesians 3:14–21. There's so much here that we are going to divide it between the petition (vv. 14–19), which is the subject of this chapter, and the doxology (vv. 20–21), which we'll study in chapter 8.

FIND YOUR STRENGTH ON YOUR KNEES

How can we afford to give up control of our lives without giving in to the trials and pressures of life? Because of our great wealth and our great worth in Jesus Christ. This is what captured Paul's attention in the early verses of Ephesians 3. He actually started to offer his prayer in verse 1, but the thought of God's gracious work among the Gentiles sent Paul into a thirteen-verse digression on the glorious revelation that had been given to him.

With all of this glorious truth flooding his heart, Paul returned to his original thought:

For this reason I bow my knees to the Father of our Lord Jesus Christ, from whom the whole family in heaven and earth is named, that He would grant you, according to the riches of His glory, to be strengthened with might through His Spirit in the inner man, that Christ may dwell in your hearts through faith. (vv. 14–17a)

Praying in Total Dependence upon God

A self-sufficient, self-satisfied man or woman will seldom pray. But a person who lives in dependence upon God, and humbly recognizes that God and God alone is the source of strength, is learning how to give up foolish self-sufficiency without giving in to circumstances or to the Enemy.

The conditions under which Paul wrote the book of Ephesians are a classic example of giving up without giving in. He wrote this letter to the Ephesians from prison, so he had given up a lot, including his freedom.

But Paul also recognized that he was not simply a prisoner of the Romans. He was "the prisoner of Christ Jesus" (Ephesians 3:1), arrested in God's will to further His kingdom. So instead of giving in to despair or bitterness, Paul's spirit was soaring as he wrote about being seated "in the heavenly places in Christ Jesus" (2:6).

Notice the humility and submission with which Paul prayed. He was on his knees before the Lord—a beautiful expression of dependence upon God. Paul was demonstrating the heart attitude of someone who has made Jesus Christ the Lord of his life. Bowing before God in prayer also acknowledges that He sovereignly reigns and rules over our lives, and that there is nowhere else we can go but to Him.

Receiving from God's Infinite Riches

If a fabulously wealthy person gave you a dollar, he would be giving *out of* his riches. But if a fabulously wealthy person gave you something *according to* his riches —that is, an amount proportionate to his wealth—you would be rich yourself.

Once you see the difference between these two types of giving, you can appreciate Ephesians 3:16, where Paul prayed that God would grant us inner strength of heart "according to the riches of His glory."

God does not simply toss us a pittance out of His great riches in Christ. He lavishes strength upon us in accordance with His infinite wealth!

Earlier, Paul called these "the unsearchable riches of Christ" (Ephesians 3:8). When you give up control to the lordship of Jesus Christ, you are coming under the authority of the Owner of the universe. There is no need you can have that He cannot supply, and in abundance.

We usually think of this in terms of our material needs, which are certainly real. Often we pray for material things while neglecting matters of the heart. But God wants us to concentrate on the inner person, because that's where the issue of control and lordship is settled. As we yield our hearts day by day to Christ, we have new inner power for living even when our outward circumstances work to weaken us and break us down.

The irony of the Christian life is that we are made strong in our weakness. We have the testimony of Paul on this:

> We are hard pressed on every side, yet not crushed; we are perplexed, but not in despair; persecuted, but not forsaken; struck down, but not destroyed—always carrying about in the body the dying of the Lord Jesus, that the life of Jesus also may be manifested in our body. For we who live are always delivered to death for Jesus' sake, that the life of Jesus also may be manifested in our mortal flesh. (2 Corinthians 4:8–11)

This incredible apostle had a catalog of suffering and trials that would bring most of us down in despair and make us give up. But as a person under the total lordship and authority of Jesus Christ, Paul had an inner strength of heart that was like reinforced steel.

Paul didn't have a corner on this kind of power, by the way. He prayed that it would be the experience of every believer. To be "strengthened with might" (Ephesians 3:16) literally means to be "empowered with power."

Because Paul had this power, he could also say despite everything that happened, "Therefore we do not lose heart. Even though our outward man is perishing, yet the inward man is being renewed day by day" (2 Corinthians 4:16). Paul was saying, "I may be growing weaker physically, but I'm getting stronger spiritually every day because the strength of Jesus Christ is my constant inner resource."

A glove is a good example of the way God's power works within us. If I lay a glove on my desk and say, "Glove, pick up my Bible," nothing will happen. The glove is absolutely helpless by itself.

But if I put my hand inside that glove and say, "Glove, pick up my Bible," the glove can respond because now it can do anything my hand can do. The power and dexterity of my hand become the power and dexterity of the glove.

In the same way, we are weak without Christ. But when His power fills us, we can do anything He asks us to do.

MAKE CHRIST AT HOME IN YOUR HEART

For me, the hinge on which Ephesians 3:14–19 turns is found in the opening phrase of verse 17. Paul prayed "that Christ may dwell in your hearts through faith." I want to spend some time looking at what it means to let Christ "dwell" in your heart.

Give Christ Full Control

Is Jesus Christ at home in your life, or is He just a visitor? Our hearts are not hotels with checkout time at noon. Our hearts and lives are meant to be royal residences for the Lord Jesus Christ.

Dwell is the key word in Ephesians 3:17. It can also be translated "be at home," which tells us that Christ is to take His place of control and comfort in your heart. When you accepted Christ as your Lord and Savior, He came to clean up, fill, control, and empower every nook and cranny of your heart. You can't shut Christ off in one room of your heart that you open only on Sunday and special religious occasions. Giving up to Christ's lordship means that He consumes and controls your entire being.

Too many of us live divided lives, with two compartments labeled "secular" and "sacred." The secular includes most of the things we do, whether it's work, school, family, or social activities.

We put our "religious" activities into the sacred or spiritual compartment. This is the area of our lives—and it's pretty small for some of us—that we reserve for church, Bible study, or whatever it may be. The so-called sacred part of life is reserved for God, but the rest of it is ours to do with as we please.

But this view of life is unbiblical. For the Christian, living under the lordship of Jesus Christ makes all of life sacred.

Paul said in Colossians 3:23, "Whatever you do, do it heartily, as to the Lord and not to men." Everything we do has to do with our relationship with Christ. I love the sign that was posted over the sink in the kitchen of a Christian camp: "Worship services held here three times daily."

When Paul talked about Christ being at home within us, he was not referring to Christ entering our hearts the first time at salvation. The issue here is the Spirit-filled life, yielding to the lordship of Christ.

For many believers, Christ is dormant within, but He's not dominant. He has a place in their hearts, but not the pre-eminence. He's a resident in the heart, but not the president.

There's a big difference between being a guest in a house and living there as a part of the family. You would probably be shocked if you discovered a houseguest looking through your dresser or sitting at your desk reading your checkbook.

But you wouldn't give it a second thought if you saw your spouse doing those things, because your spouse has the right of access to every part of your home and life. Jesus Christ purchased us for Himself when He paid for our sins on the cross. He has the right of access to every part of our lives.

Live for Christ's Pleasure

It's our responsibility to do everything we can to make sure that Jesus Christ is not a stranger or merely a guest in our hearts. He is not an add-on to our existence; He *is* our existence.

One of my favorite heroes was Eric Liddell, the subject of the Academy-Award winning film *Chariots of Fire.* Liddell was a committed Scottish believer who went to the mission field in China after his gold medal performance in the 1924 Olympics. Liddell was imprisoned by the Japanese in China during World War II, and he died in a concentration camp in 1945.

There is a memorable scene early in *Chariots of Fire,* in which Eric was talking with his sister Jenny, who was chastising him for his pursuit of athletics. She urged Eric to give up his track career and devote himself more fully to the call of Christ upon his life. Eric responded, "I know that God made me for China. But He also made me fast, and when I run I feel His pleasure."

Your circumstances may not be as dramatic as Eric Liddell's, but you ought to be able to say, "When I go to school, I feel God's pleasure." "When I do my work, I feel God's pleasure." "When I play with my children, I feel God's pleasure." To feel His pleasure in what you do is to make Him at home in your heart.

This means that all things are to be done to God's glory. "Whether you eat or drink, or whatever you do, do all to the glory of God" (1 Corinthians 10:31). A good motto for life is all things for God's praise, all things for God's purposes, and all things for God's pleasure.

It needs to be said again: When you yield your life to Christ and give up the control of your heart, you're not giving in to life. As a matter of fact, it's when you give up that you discover God's best. Your life becomes productive.

I can prove this from Romans 12:1–2. Paul urged us to present our bodies to Christ as living sacrifices and to allow Him to transform us, the result being that "you may prove what is that good and acceptable and perfect will of God."

Life doesn't get any better than knowing and doing God's will. We experience sweet rest and overflowing joy. Prayer becomes powerful. The Bible explodes in our hearts. Our witness spreads throughout our daily walk, and life becomes joyful, pleasurable, and powerful.

How? Because we are "filled with all the fullness of God" (Ephesians 3:19), and Jesus Christ begins to reproduce His abundant life in us.

Open Every Room to Christ

Do you have any secret closets in your heart? These could be pet sins or private thoughts that you reserve for yourself, or an area of disobedience. Jesus Christ cannot be completely at home in your heart until you are ready to give Him the key to those closets.

A number of years ago, a pastor named Robert

Munger delivered a sermon entitled "My Heart, Christ's Home." This message was put into a little booklet of the same name that has become a Christian classic.

In this message, Munger described the human heart as a home with many rooms, and he imagined Christ coming in to make His home in the heart. As He moves through each room, Christ begins to deal with the things He finds there.

As He enters the home of the heart, the Lord goes into the library, the place of our thoughts. When He looks at what the person has been feeding into his mind, the homeowner becomes uncomfortable. When he admits he needs to alter things, Christ offers to help in the process.

Then Christ moves into the dining room, the place where we fulfill our appetites. The heart's owner realizes that Christ doesn't touch any of the food he has offered, because it is all worldly fare and dissatisfying to the soul.

Next, Christ goes with the homeowner into the living room. There they sit by the fire and talk and make an appointment to come daily to stop long enough to have a conversation. But several days later the homeowner walks by the room to see to his surprise that Jesus is sitting there waiting to meet with him—and has been doing so every morning.

Then Jesus goes to the workshop and asks the homeowner to show Him what he's been doing there. The owner shows a few little toys and trinkets he has made. Jesus offers to take the homeowner's hands and make better, more useful things through him.

Then one day Jesus is walking up the stairs of the man's heart and says, "There is a peculiar odor in the house. There is something dead around here. It's upstairs . . . in the hall closet."

By now the man is getting a little perturbed. Jesus has already taken over his living room, his kitchen, his library, and his workroom. This is just a little closet where he keeps a few things for himself.

But Jesus cannot live in the same house with the putrid odor, so the homeowner reluctantly offers the key, saying as he does that Jesus will need to clean the closet out Himself, because he lacks the strength. Jesus opens the closet and a foul stench comes out from unconfessed and unrepented secret sins. Jesus takes the cleansing power of His love and grace and cleans out all of that garbage.

Then the homeowner realizes what has been happening and says, "Lord, you have been a guest, and I have been the host. From now on I am going to be the servant. You are going to be the Lord." And to show his sincerity, he runs, gets the deed to the house, and signs it over to Christ.

Somehow people today have the idea that becoming a follower of Jesus Christ means simply adding Him to the list of their other activities and interests. But the answer to the question, "If I give Christ control of my heart, is He going to change things?" is *absolutely* . . . but always for the better!

My friend, fellow pastor, and conference speaker Greg Laurie has a great way of illustrating this truth—something of an updated version of Robert Munger's idea.

Greg says that when Jesus Christ comes into your life, He starts tearing up that old shag carpet you've had since the 1960s, then throws out old lava lamp and your beat-up furniture. You say, "Lord, You've taken away all the things I've collected over the years! What am I going to do now?"

But about that time a big moving van pulls up outside. On the van is the name "Father and Son Moving Company." In walk two holy angels with brand-new carpet, new paint for the walls, and beautiful new furniture. Everything is laid out exquisitely.

It's another way of saying that, when Jesus Christ takes control of a life, "Old things have passed away; behold, all things have become new" (2 Corinthians 5:17).

GET YOUR MIND
AROUND GOD'S GREAT LOVE

When the lordship of Jesus Christ is firmly established in your heart, you're ready to experience the fullness of His love. Here's how Paul described it as he continued his great prayer in Ephesians 3:

> For this reason I bow my knees to the Father of our Lord Jesus Christ . . . that you, being rooted and grounded in love, may be able to comprehend with all the saints what is the width and length and depth and height—to know the love of Christ which passes knowledge; that you may be filled with all the fullness of God. (vv. 14, 17b–19)

Comprehending the Incomprehensible

One of the benefits of giving up to Christ, without giving in to the world, is that God pours His love into our hearts (see Romans 5:5). Now if the greatest love in the universe is living within you, the best thing you can do is try to grasp the greatness of that love.

That's what Paul meant when he prayed that we would "comprehend" the love God has for us. That word means to "seize," to grab hold of this love and grow in it day by day.

When my wife, Deb, and I were married more than thirty years ago, I was certain I couldn't love anybody as much as I loved her at that moment. And like most newlyweds, I was certain that I already comprehended all that our love could mean.

But as Deb and I have grown together in the soulmate experience of marriage, my love for her is greater today than it was when we married. I have seized her love more and have known and experienced it more than I possibly could have imagined on our wedding day.

What is true of marriage is true to an even greater degree in our relationship with Jesus Christ. When we first taste His love, it seems that we have reached the heights of heaven. But as we grow and experience the presence of God, we experience and understand more and more of His love.

Measuring the Immeasurable

God's love reaches out in infinite ways and in every dimension, from width to length to depth to height.

How wide is God's love? So wide that it reaches around the world and embraces all people. When Jesus reached out His arms on the cross, the arms of God wrapped around the whole world. His love is as wide as the world.

How long is the love of God? It reaches from eternity past to eternity present to eternity future. Before the stars were formed His love was there, and after the stars have fallen the love of God will remain forever.

How deep is God's love? Deep enough to reach to the depths of sin and rescue the lowest sinner. No matter how depraved or evil a person may be, God's love can reach down to lift that person out of the mire. I always think of what the late Corrie ten Boom said after surviving a Nazi concentration camp. "There is no pit so deep that He is not deeper still." If God's love is deep enough to sustain His people in the most horrifying suffering imaginable, you and I don't have to worry about reaching the bottom of His grace.

How high is the love of God? It is so high that it reaches all the way into the heavenly places (Ephesians 1:3, 20; 2:6). When we come to Christ, we are lifted up with Him into heaven and seated there with Him.

The bottom line is that God's love for us is beyond our ability to comprehend or measure. So don't worry if you're having a hard time getting your mind around the greatness of Christ's love for you. Paul himself said this love "passes knowledge." We will spend a lifetime, and then all of eternity, uncovering the extent of God's love and learning to love Him.

Giving up without giving in doesn't mean surrender or defeat but overwhelming victory. Are you ready for the challenge of a lifetime? Then give up to Christ and enthrone Him as Lord of your heart.

Chapter Eight

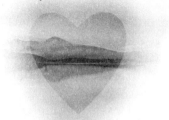

TO GOD
BE THE
GLORY

*T*he Christian world has been taken by storm with the publication of a small book that carries the unlikely title *The Prayer of Jabez*. This best-seller has become the focus of widespread attention and discussion, catapulting Jabez from the status of an obscure Old Testament character to a household word.

Who was Jabez, and what was it about his prayer that has caused thousands of Christians to make it part of their daily prayer lives? The book's author, Bruce Wilkinson, says that Jabez's prayer in 1 Chronicles 4:10 is a model of believing prayer that we can learn from and imitate today as we seek God's blessing on our lives. Jabez was a man from the tribe of Judah who appears in Scripture for a grand total of two verses (1 Chronicles 4:9–10) in the middle of a very long genealogy.

First Chronicles 1–9 is one of those sections of the Bible that most people hurry through since it's little more than a catalog of names. Jabez's name appears on the list as the Bible says about him, "Jabez was more honorable than his brothers."

That's worth noting in itself, but what makes Jabez leap off the page and stand out among all the other names is the daring prayer he prayed. "Oh, that You would bless me indeed, and enlarge my territory, that Your hand would be with me, and that You would keep me from evil" (v. 10). On the surface, this looks like a selfish prayer. Here's a man praying, "Dear God, pour out Your blessings on me and enlarge the sphere of my life."

But the amazing thing is what follows: "So God granted him what he requested." The way God answered Jabez's prayer gives us the encouragement and the boldness to pray in the same way.

Jesus said, "Ask, and it will be given to you" (Matthew 7:7). James challenged us with these words: "You do not have because you do not ask" (James 4:2). The fact is that God wants to take ordinary people who believe in Him and do extraordinary things through them in answer to their prayers. That way, when it's all said and done, all of the glory, praise, and honor will go to Him.

You can't find anyone more ordinary than Jabez. He might have disappeared into the dustbin of biblical history like most of the people mentioned in that genealogy, except for one thing: Jabez understood that he served an extraordinary God, who was able to do above and beyond anything he could ask, and he asked God in faith to pour out His blessings.

Does that sound like a health-and-wealth gospel? It's not, because the apostle Paul made the same point in Ephesians 3:20–21, the benediction to one of the Bible's greatest prayers. The context of this prayer is crucial, because Paul was not praying for material wealth but for God's will and purpose for His people. The bottom line is that you can live an abundant life, blessed by the favor of

God, when the unswerving purpose of your heart is to praise Him and seek His eternal glory.

The apostle was not quite halfway through his letter to the church at Ephesus when the reality of God's glory and power overwhelmed him. Paul went to his knees in prayer, asking God to enable believers to grow strong in faith and be filled with God's power and fullness (3:14–19).

Then Paul concluded his prayer with a doxology of praise—a beautiful expression of faith for any child of God who dares to pray like this: "Now to Him who is able to do exceedingly abundantly above all that we ask or think, according to the power that works in us, to Him be glory in the church by Christ Jesus to all generations, forever and ever. Amen" (Ephesians 3:20–21).

If these verses are familiar to you, you may want to take a minute to let each word register in your mind and heart. The Bible says we can expect and receive from God more blessings than we could possibly imagine to carry out His will here on earth and live full, abundant lives.

The abundant life was promised to us when Jesus said, "I have come that they may have life, and that they may have it more abundantly" (John 10:10). This life is provided for us by the same infinite power that raised Jesus from the dead.

Living an abundant life means that we can rise above our circumstances and get a vision that's bigger than our own world. When our hearts are centered on God's praise and glory, when our deepest desire is "to God be the glory in everything," our lives can be revolutionized.

Ephesians 3:20–21 is a prayer powerhouse when we come to God in a way that pleases Him. But there are at least three conditions we must fulfill in order to experience the power and blessings of God, so that we might bring Him glory.

WE MUST ASK WITH A CHRIST-CENTERED FOCUS

God's promise of blessings "above all that we ask or think" is not thrown out haphazardly for us to grab and use for our own pleasure and ease. The apostle James warned that self-centered petitions have no impact in heaven. "You ask and do not receive, because you ask amiss, that you may spend it on your pleasures" (James 4:3).

The opposite of asking with a self-centered focus is to ask with a Christ-centered focus. That doesn't necessarily mean that we pray only for "spiritual" things. The Bible invites us to make our needs known to God and expect great things from Him.

Praying with a Christ-centered focus simply means that whatever He wants for you is what you want for yourself. You can bring any request to God in a spirit of expectancy when the commitment of your heart is to honor Him with everything you have and everything you are.

Daring to Trust God

When was the last time you prayed a prayer that was so daring, so bold, and so big that you would be left in the lurch if God didn't answer—or if God did answer, it would be so astounding that it would be obvious only God could have done it? I'm not talking about tempting or daring God but trusting Him for the power, the strength, and the resources to do something that's far beyond our ability in ourselves. If I understand Ephesians 3:20 correctly, we don't have to worry about bringing God a request that's beyond Him. His ability to bless us is far beyond our greatest imagination.

But, as Bruce Wilkinson pooints out in *Prayer of Jabez,* today the concept of God's blessing has basically been reduced to a superstitious catchphrase people say when someone sneezes. "God bless you." Or people use these words as little more than the equivalent of "Have a nice day."

Is that all the blessing of God involves? In the Bible, to be blessed of God means that His mighty hand is moving in your behalf, the favor of God is upon you, and His supernatural power is within you. The blessing of God is His unlimited grace and goodness. Yet I wonder how many of us are missing blessings from God because our concept of Him is too small.

There's a fable about a man who died and went to heaven. He was being ushered around on the streets of gold and shown the beautiful mansions of glory when he came upon a big warehouse. He asked the angel escorting him, "What's in that warehouse?"

The angel said, "You don't want to know what's in there."

But the man insisted. "Oh, I certainly do. This is heaven, and there are no secrets here. I want to know what's in that warehouse."

"Well, if you insist," the angel replied. He took the man inside to a huge room stacked with boxes and crates all the way to the ceiling, as far as the eye could see.

The man noticed that there was a name on every box, so he asked the angel, "Do I have a box in here?" The angel assured him that he did, and the man rushed to find it. Sure enough, he found a huge box with his name on it.

"What's in my box?" he asked the angel.

"Your box contains all the blessings God wanted to give you while you were on earth, but which you failed to ask and believe Him for. This box has been here forever with your name on it, with all of the blessings inside reserved for you. But you never received them because you didn't dare to believe that God would give you so much more than you imagined."

Are there blessings reserved in heaven for you that are going unclaimed because you never asked? Some Christians say, "Well, I've already been given so much more than I deserve that it just doesn't seem right to ask for more blessings."

We've *all* been given far more than we deserve—all we really deserve is judgment! But do you think God wants to stop now with His blessings? Listen to Paul's compelling argument in Romans 8:32. "He who did not spare His own Son, but delivered Him up for us all, how shall He not with Him also freely give us all things?"

Would you dare to ask God for the rich resources that are always available to you in Christ? The difference between asking for personal greed and asking for God's praise and glory is in the attitude of our hearts.

We always need to be on guard against harboring wrong motives. But when our goal is to honor Christ and bring Him glory, we can ask largely.

Praising in Spite of Prison

Our focus makes all the difference in our praying. Remember that as Paul wrote these words he was in prison. But he turned his prison house into a church house by turning his focus upward to the Lord. Centering our hearts on Christ can turn a prison stint into a praise service. That's what it did for Paul.

One day a man passed by a group of workmen building a church. He asked the first workman what he was doing. "I'm pouring cement," came the answer.

The man asked the second worker the same question. "I'm laying bricks."

Then the passerby asked the third worker what he was doing. "Oh," he said with a smile, "I'm building a cathedral for the worship and praise of God."

That was Paul's perspective. He got on his knees and looked to heaven, so instead of seeing prison walls he saw a God who was infinitely greater than his circumstances.

We need that same vision to be set before us as God's people. I often tell the people of our church in Plano that our vision is not of buildings or a bigger membership roll. Our vision as a church is to bow down in humble adoration and dependence upon God, with grateful acceptance of all that He has done and all that we have been given in Christ. And then our vision is to pray that He would bless us even more.

The secret of growth for any church is to lift up Jesus Christ. He is the attracting power and personality of the church. When we set our focus upon Him and He is lifted up, we won't have to worry about how to get people in the doors.

As a pastor, I learned a long time ago that it's not my responsibility to make sure there are people in the house but to see that Jesus is in the house, because when He is in the house, He's going to draw people unto Himself.

WE MUST ASK WITH A CHRIST-CENTERED FAITH

The writer of Hebrews said, "He who comes to God must believe that He is, and that He is a rewarder of those who diligently seek Him" (Hebrews 11:6). God is looking for people who believe Him so He can bless them!

Looking for Someone Who Believes

God's capacity to bless is beyond question, but to a certain extent He has shut Himself up to our faith. I can give you a guarantee that God's blessing upon your life can be abundant and available to you beginning this very moment.

How can I make this guarantee? Because God's Word says that His blessings have already been promised and provided. We forget sometimes that it is God's nature and desire to bless us. We are not wrestling with a reluctant deity who gives grudgingly. God wants to pour out His blessings upon us.

The Bible makes an amazing statement in 2 Chronicles 16:9. "The eyes of the Lord run to and fro throughout the whole earth, to show Himself strong on behalf of those whose heart is loyal to Him."

Part of our problem is that we think the blessings of God must be for other people—the wealthy, the smart, the strong, or the important. But you'll notice that none of these criteria comes into play when God is looking for someone to bless. Instead, He's looking for faithfulness. "It is required in stewards that one be found faithful" (1 Corinthians 4:2). If you are a believer, you don't have to be any of these other things if you are a faithful person who believes God in your heart and acts upon that belief. You can be blessed with the abundant provision of God to see His will accomplished in your heart and life.

Now let me repeat my earlier caution. We cannot stand up in God's face and demand whatever we want, whether it's in His will or not. God is not obligated to act at our bidding just because we "name it and claim it."

But the problem with most Christians is that they don't believe and don't ask, and therefore they don't receive from God what He desires to give them. The Bible doesn't say that those who come to God must have it all together or be able to demonstrate their strength and abilities and connections. In fact, God can't bless us if we think we can do it all and don't need any help.

But when we bow in humble dependence upon God, admitting that we can't but He can, confessing that we're not able but He is, then He can do amazing things through us and trust us with abundant blessings.

When was the last time you asked God to act exceedingly abundantly on your behalf? Do you believe God still performs miracles? I do!

Apparently some Christians think God has gotten older now and can't do what He used to do. He did things in the old days, but not today. However, the Scripture says,

"Jesus Christ is the same yesterday, today, and forever" (Hebrews 13:8).

Talk to some Christians about God's work in their lives, and you get a history lesson. Everything is past tense, what God used to do. Maybe this is true because they've forgotten that God wants to bless His people in a fresh way every day. His mercies "are new every morning" (Lamentations 3:23).

God wants to bless you right where you are, for His glory, but you must be willing to exercise the kind of faith that isn't afraid to take a risk. I think a lot of us want to hedge our bets, to play life safely so we don't get too far out on a limb where it would demand radical faith of us.

But let's be willing to take some risks of faith that are so big and so daring from our perspective, that if God doesn't come through we're finished. God is looking for some individuals and churches willing to trust Him in a big way.

The line between faith and presumption can be a fine one, so the question naturally comes up, How do you know when you have crossed the line? There is no "one size fits all" answer, but with prayer, wise counsel from others, and some sanctified common sense, it's possible to discern when you are tempting God instead of trusting Him.

The Unlimited Power Available to Us

God's ability to do far more than we can ask or think is tied to "the power that works in us" (Ephesians 3:20). Paul explained this power a little earlier in Ephesians, in the middle of another dynamic prayer the apostle prayed for believers. This time he asked that God would give us "the spirit of wisdom and revelation" and open our spiritual eyes so that we would know some important truths (Ephesians 1:15–18).

Among these truths is "the exceeding greatness of His power toward us who believe, according to the working of

His mighty power which He worked in Christ when He raised Him from the dead and seated Him at His right hand in the heavenly places" (vv. 19–20).

Did you read that carefully? The power that is available to us today, and is actually *at work* in us, is the same power that raised Jesus Christ from the dead. This is resurrection power, but notice that it goes beyond the power necessary to bring Jesus back to life. God not only raised His Son from the dead but raised Him up to heaven.

Now you know why Paul had no reservation at all in saying that God is abundantly able to do far beyond anything we can imagine. The secret isn't the size of our faith, but the greatness of our God. We can't outdream God, outask God, or expect more than God can give.

The book of Acts is the story of the way the church exploded in the first century. Here in the twenty-first century, I believe the principles for God's work are the same because God is the same and His power is undiminished. Acts 11:21 describes that power at work: "The hand of the Lord was with them, and a great number believed and turned to the Lord." There is no reason that this can't be said about the church today. We have the same power and potential at our fingertips. Our faith in Christ links us with His power to accomplish His work.

A little boy and his father were walking in a field one day when they stopped for a few minutes. Wanting to show his father how strong he was, the boy went up to a large rock and began trying to move it. He grunted and strained, but the rock didn't budge. Seeing a chance to teach his son a valuable lesson, the father said, "Son, you're not using all the strength you have to move that rock." Accepting this as a challenge, the boy started working harder, but only grew more frustrated as the rock refused to move.

Dad watched the struggle for a few more minutes and then said again, "Son, you're not using all the power you have to move that rock."

"Yes I am, Daddy!" cried the frustrated youngster.

This went on several more times, until the boy was exhausted and almost in tears. His father knelt by him and said tenderly, "Son, you're not using all the strength available to you to move that rock. You haven't asked me to move it for you." And the father easily moved the rock.

Let's not be guilty of grunting and groaning in our finite weakness while failing to ask in faith for the help of our infinitely able God.

WE MUST ASK WITH
CHRIST-CENTERED FUTURE PLANS

Here's a third condition to fulfill that will allow us to experience the power and blessings of God. If our focus and our faith are centered in Christ, it won't be hard for us to commit our future to Him.

A Lasting Legacy of Faith

Any investment you make in the kingdom of God and the church of Jesus Christ is the most secure investment you can make, because it is laid up in store for eternity in heaven where nothing can touch it (see Matthew 6:19–21).

Paul's great prayer ends with this doxology: "Unto him be glory in the church by Christ Jesus throughout all ages, world without end. Amen" (Ephesians 3:21 KJV). We could also say, "To Him be glory throughout all generations." A lasting legacy is suggested here, one that reaches from generation to generation. To our children and our children's children, victory in Christ is secure. The promises of God are forever.

Some wag looked at our increasingly violent, dangerous, and polluted world, with all of its political upheavals and fluctuations in the financial markets, and quipped, "The future ain't what it used to be." That's a clever line, but I have to differ with this conclusion. When you live to give God glory, your future is *better* than it used to be because it is as secure as the power and promises of God.

People talk about wanting to go with a winner. Here's a sure thing to stake your future on. Jesus said, "I will build my church, and the gates of Hades shall not prevail against it" (Matthew 16:18).

The church of Jesus Christ is the best and only hope for this nation and the world. Why? Because the church alone carries the message and the mission of Jesus. Make sure your future is securely tied to Christ.

The Best Is Yet to Be

John Erskine was a brilliant university professor, the author of sixty books, a concert pianist, and a popular lecturer. But students at Columbia University flocked to Erskine's classes not just because of his fame and accomplishments, but because of what he believed about them. Erskine regularly told his students, "The best books are yet to be written. The best paintings are yet to be painted. The best governments are yet to be formed. The best is yet to be done by you."

That's what God is saying to us. If all the great work God wants to do has already been done, we might as well turn out the lights and go home. But it's still true that, with God, great things are always still ahead.

Don't misunderstand. God gave us His best when Jesus died for us on the cross, and that will never be improved upon. But there are always greater challenges ahead for us. Our future is bright when we anchor our future in Him.

When I was pastor of the First Baptist Church in West Palm Beach, Florida, I was looking around in a hallway of the church one day and found a battered old pulpit that had been stuffed in a closet. It was actually a preaching rail with a small lectern. I asked around to find out about this interesting piece of furniture. Someone told me it was the church's original pulpit and that there was an incredible story behind it.

It seems that in 1928, a huge hurricane hit the Gulf Coast of Florida and blew the church apart. It was on the ground, with boards, lumber, and bricks everywhere. The only thing left standing was that pulpit. More than that, the older people claimed that a Bible was found lying intact on the pulpit, opened to Isaiah 40:8, "The grass withereth, the flower fadeth: but the word of our God shall stand for ever" (KJV).

That pulpit withstanding the storm is a great picture of believers whose focus is upon the Lord, whose faith is in Him, and whose future is anchored in Him. When we are determined to live for God's glory and accept nothing less than all He has for us, we'll be standing even when everything else around us has collapsed.

Chapter Nine

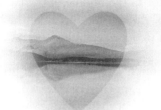

THE HEART OF
AUTHENTIC
WORSHIP

*O*ne of the most respected theologians in evangelical Christianity has made some disturbing observations about the quality of worship in the contemporary church:

> Evangelical Protestantism is in trouble today. . . . The complaint I hear most often is that people can no longer sense the sacred. . . . The atmosphere in most of our services is clubby and convivial rather than adoring and expectant. What is missing is the fear of God, the experience of God as the Wholly Other. Worship has become performance rather than praise.[1]

These are strong words, but many Christians would have to admit that they ring true. Legions of people are coming to church every Sunday, going through the motions of worship, mouthing words of praise and adoration to God, and yet going home with their hearts unchanged.

Capturing the heart of true worship is a challenge the

church faces in every generation. A. W. Tozer, a great Christian author in the middle of the twentieth century, called worship "the missing jewel" of the church. If it is, then we ought to do everything we can to rediscover this jewel.

Why do church services that offer little more than a "clubby" environment fail to satisfy us or honor God? The answer lies in the fact that we were created with the capacity to know God and experience His presence and to return unto Him worship that is worthy of Him.

Nothing less than God-honoring, God-exalting worship can fill the longing in our hearts to commune with Him. The psalmist declared, "I will praise You, O Lord, with my whole heart" (Psalm 9:1). We sing a powerful little chorus that expresses well the heart of true worship:

> *I'm coming back to the heart of worship,*
> *For it's all about You, It's all about You.*
> *I'm sorry Lord for the thing I've made it,*
> *When it's all about You, It's all about You, Jesus.*[2]

WORSHIP MUST BE A PRIORITY

The Bible makes clear that worship is a priority issue. The first commandment that God gave His people concerned their worship. "I am the Lord your God, who brought you out of the land of Egypt, out of the house of bondage. You shall have no other gods before Me" (Exodus 20:2–3). The second commandment then forbade the making and worship of idols.

God Looks at Our Hearts

Worship involves what we do both with our hearts and with our hands. There are inward and outward components to worship, but the essence of real worship is the attitude of our hearts.

Jesus Himself summarized the commandments dealing with our relationship to God by saying, "You shall love the Lord your God with all your heart, with all your soul, with all your mind, and with all your strength" (Mark 12:30).

The way we express our love for God is to worship Him. But we know from Israel's history, and from the experience of the church, that it's possible to carry out the forms of worship while the worshipers' hearts are far from God.

Israel fell into that ditch a number of times, and God had something definite to say about it: "These people draw near with their mouths and honor Me with their lips, but have removed their hearts far from Me" (Isaiah 29:13).

God also told the people through the prophet Amos, "Though you offer Me burnt offerings and your grain offerings, I will not accept them" (Amos 5:22). God rejected Judah's acts of worship because the people's hearts were full of injustice and unrighteousness (see v. 24).

God Made Us for Worship

God created us to be His worshipers. He desires and deserves our worship, offered from hearts that are deeply in love with Him.

The Bible is saturated with worship from beginning to end. Worship was the first activity of God's first created beings. God created the angels before time began, and worship has always been their chief occupation. Many Bible commentators believe that before Lucifer sinned and became Satan, his responsibility in heaven was to lead the angels in the worship of God.

Worship is the eternal focus of the angels, it was the priority command for the people of Israel, and it is the call of God upon every Christian today. The church has four primary purposes, which are worship, teaching, evangelism, and service.

These are what the church is and does. Each is important, but at the very top of the list is worship. Before we witness or work, and even before the Word of God is proclaimed, we are to worship our great God.

One indication of the priority of worship is that it's the only part of the church's mission as we know it here on earth that we will still be doing in heaven. There will be no need for preaching in heaven. I'll be out of a job in glory!

We won't pray in heaven because we will know even as we are known. There is no witness or evangelism in heaven, for the day of salvation will be past. And a large part of the church's work on earth—teaching the Word, encouraging believers, comforting the bereaved, counseling the confused, providing for financial needs, and so forth —will not be necessary in heaven.

But throughout all of eternity, we will continue to praise and glorify and magnify God. We will worship in heaven! That's why it's sad that so many individual Christians and churches have not discovered authentic worship. If our worship is limited or out of focus, let's get it together down here, because it will be our eternal occupation.

The Living God Wants to Meet Us

For too many believers, church means services as usual. I think it's time for us to have some services as *un*usual, because the living God wants to meet with us in worship.

People say they've been in boring worship services, but that's not really true. They may have been in some boring *church* services. But how can it be boring to be in the presence of God Almighty as you truly worship Him? It is impossible to be bored in the presence of the God of heaven.

So the key is to make sure that when we worship, we come to exalt, extol, and honor the Lord. This is the goal whether we are worshiping in God's house with other believers or in the privacy of our own devotions. God's presence is manifest in any place where He is worshiped.

A wonderful mystery takes place in worship, but worship itself is not mysterious in terms of what God expects from us. God's Word reveals the elements involved in worship that pleases Him.

We could turn to many passages of Scripture for instruction on worship. The Bible says more about worship than about prayer, witnessing, or service. Worship begins in the opening chapters of Genesis, when God made Adam and Eve to walk in intimate fellowship with Him, and it climaxes in the book of Revelation with God's people in His presence forever.

As a matter of fact, the longest book in the Bible is devoted primarily to the worship of God. Psalms is the hymnbook and worship manual of Scripture, expressing praise, adoration, and glory to the Lord. I want to tap into this wealth by examining Psalm 34:1–5, tremendous verses that give us some valuable insights on authentic worship.

WORSHIP REQUIRES PERSONAL INVOLVEMENT

The first thing I want us to see is that worship is an intensely personal act that demands the participation of our total being. David wrote, "*I* will bless the Lord at all times; His praise shall continually be in *my* mouth" (Psalm 34:1, italics added).

If I asked you whether you went to church last Sunday, you could answer right away. You either did or didn't attend. But if I asked whether you worshiped God last Sunday, that might require some thought before you could answer. The reason is that worship is far more than just showing up at church with a Bible in our hands.

We Are Participants, Not Spectators

The problem with the church today is that we have taken our worship cues from our entertainment-oriented culture. The result is that worship has become largely a spectator sport.

I'm reminded of the classic description that the late great coach Bud Wilkinson gave of football. "Football is 50,000 people in the stands desperately in need of exercise, watching 22 people on the field desperately in need of rest."

Worship is like that in many churches. We tend to think of the pastors, worship leaders, and singers as the performers doing their job on the platform, while the congregation enjoys and responds to the show like spectators at a ball game. God is the prompter in heaven, giving the performers their lines to deliver from the platform.

But authentic worship is not built on an entertainment model. The pastors, musicians, and worship leaders guide the collective body of Christ in worshiping and adoring God, and they help the people direct their praise to the One who is worthy. The leaders also teach and remind the people of God's goodness and glory, enhancing their ability to worship in spirt and in truth.

It's amazing to think that God attends to our worship. You can't send someone else to worship for you—but why would you want to? When you realize that worship brings you into the presence of your heavenly Father, who loves you and seeks your best, then worshiping Him ought to become your highest goal.

When the famous naturalist John Muir visited California's Yosemite Valley in the 1860s, his reports of its beauty aroused a lot of interest and led eventually to the establishment of Yosemite National Park in 1890.

Muir wanted others to experience the awesome surroundings of Yosemite for themselves. So in 1903, he took

President Theodore Roosevelt camping in Yosemite, giving Roosevelt a firsthand look at the park's beauty. It was then that Roosevelt became a passionate advocate for conservation.

You cannot become a passionate worshiper without firsthand participation. King David knew the value of worship. This great leader lived an incredible life. He was a teenaged hero in Israel, he experienced the heights of kingly glory, and he also tasted deep sorrow and heartbreak. He sinned greatly, only to repent and discover God's great grace and forgiveness.

Looking back on his life and all that had happened to him, David recorded the one thing that mattered more to him than anything else: "One thing I have desired of the Lord, that will I seek: that I may dwell in the house of the Lord all the days of my life, to behold the beauty of the Lord, and to inquire in His temple" (Psalm 27:4).

David wrote that because he was also a great worshiper, the "sweet psalmist of Israel" (2 Samuel 23:1). This was the secret to his life. So when it came down to what was most important, David could say, "More than anything else, I want to be in God's house and in His presence, beholding His beauty and pouring out my heart in worship to Him."

Worship Is a Magnificent Witness

Wonderful things happen when we worship God. Jesus said, "I, if I am lifted up from the earth, will draw all peoples to Myself" (John 12:32). This was speaking of the crucifixion, but we lift up Christ in a different way when we gather to worship Him, and this becomes a powerful witnessing tool to unbelievers.

People who don't know Christ know nothing of what real worship is. Unbelievers don't usually even sing together in groups, unless it's at a ballgame where they join in the national anthem.

Yet, when an unbeliever comes into an environment in which Christ is lifted up and worshiped from the heart, that person is unmistakably and irresistibly drawn by the Spirit and Word of God to Jesus Christ.

This doesn't mean that worship is a substitute for our personal witness. It is the other side of the coin of witnessing. There is something attractive and arresting about authentic worship that has a powerful effect on lost people. Evangelism may not be the primary reason the church gathers for worship, but unsaved people are often brought under conviction of their sin in an atmosphere of worship. I've seen it happen many times.

Worship Is Our Unique Privilege

Personal worship is part of the unique privilege given to us as human beings. The animal and plant kingdoms don't know the privilege of worshiping God.

During Jesus' triumphal entry into Jerusalem on His way to the cross, His disciples spread their clothes on the ground and waved branches, shouting praises to God. Some Pharisees were offended by this and called out to Jesus, "Teacher, rebuke Your disciples" (Luke 19:39).

But Jesus gave a very interesting response. "I tell you that if these should keep silent, the stones would immediately cry out" (v. 40). God was going to see to it that Jesus Christ received the worship due Him at that moment, even if He had to use objects of nature. However, Jesus' disciples exercised their privilege of worship, and a miracle like that wasn't necessary.

I have a beagle at home that is almost human. But I've never seen my beagle go outside in the yard, get down on his knees, raise his front paws, and bark out praises to God. Animals don't have the capacity for worship that God has given us.

The Bible says, "He has put eternity in [our] hearts"

(Ecclesiastes 3:11). We have the capacity to break through to the eternal—to know and experience God in worship. The fact that unbelievers pervert worship through idolatry and false religions is evidence of the unquenchable thirst God has put in our hearts to worship something beyond ourselves.

God Seeks Authentic Worshipers

Does it astonish you to realize that the God of heaven, the Creator of all things, is actually looking for people to worship Him with authenticity? He is! We know this because of Jesus' conversation with the Samaritan woman at the well, during which He said something that startles me every time I read it.

This woman tried to draw Jesus into the controversy of the day over the proper place to worship God. But Jesus told her, "The hour is coming, and now is, when the true worshipers will worship the Father in spirit and truth; *for the Father is seeking such to worship Him*" (John 4:23, italics added).

Someone may say, "Why does God want our worship? How can anything we say and do add anything to a God who is already perfect?" God doesn't seek our worship because He is deficient in any way or because He has an ego that needs bolstering. The privilege in worship is ours. In His glory, greatness, grandeur, and grace, God grants us an opportunity to know Him and express our love through worship.

Jesus said the kind of worship God wants is "in spirit," worship that flows from our affections and from heartfelt adoration. It's interesting that one of the most common words in the New Testament for worship means "to kiss toward," which speaks of bowing or prostrating ourselves before God.

Authentic worship is an expression of love and adoration that comes from our inner person. Jesus said we are also to worship "in truth." That is, our worship must be informed by the Word of God, which tells us who and how we're to worship.

Many worshipers in the world today are bowing down to false gods. But it's only when we worship the true God in light of His truth that we connect with Him.

The Power of Expressing Praise

The Bible calls us to articulate and openly express our worship to God. Notice the second half of Psalm 34:1 once again. "His praise shall continually be in my mouth."

We know how important it is for husbands and wives to express their love for each other. Sometimes a wife may wonder if her husband really loves her, because he never tells her. One wife asked her husband, "Why don't you ever tell me that you love me?"

His response was, "On the day we got married I told you that I loved you. If anything changes, I'll let you know."

That's not how real love works, and it's not how worship works, either. A vital part of worship is verbally and publicly expressing our praises to God.

Private worship is wonderful. I've had deep, life-changing experiences alone with God. But although worship is at times private and deeply personal, it is also to be public and vocal. The writer of Hebrews spoke of offering "the sacrifice of praise to God, that is, the fruit of our lips, giving thanks to His name" (Hebrews 13:15). This is verbalized praise that goes up to God as a sweet-smelling offering.

Paul and Silas sang out in praise to God in the jail at Philippi (Acts 16:25), and the jailer got saved. Had the apostles only worshiped God in the privacy of their hearts, this man might have never known who Jesus was and how he could be saved.

WORSHIP HAS A DEFINITE SHAPE

Authentic worship is not a series of warm, shapeless feelings floating in the air. The world may be into aromatherapy sessions and enacting pagan rituals in the forest, but the Bible defines the parameters of real worship. Since worship that pleases God is firmly anchored in truth, we can discover the content of worship in His Word.

Our Worship Must Be True to Scripture

For worship to be authentic, it has to correspond to what is revealed about God in Scripture. Ascribing blessing and praise to God because He is worthy is part of truth-related worship. We adore Him because He is worthy of all praise. Blessing God reveals His "worth-ship," which is the Anglo-Saxon word for worship. We normally think of God blessing us. But in worship, we bless the Blesser.

The Bible consistently ties our worship of God to His divine attributes. The truth of who God is in the perfections of His deity is rapidly being lost on this generation. That's why the most important thing we can do today is to rediscover God as He is, not as who we would like Him to be.

David also revealed the content of worship in Psalm 29 when he wrote, "Give unto the Lord glory and strength. Give unto the Lord the glory due to His name. Worship the Lord in the beauty of holiness" (vv. 1–2). This is important because we must grasp the reality of God's greatness and majesty before we can worship Him in spirit and in truth.

Psalm 29:1–2 gives us something close to a definition of authentic worship. In its essence, worship is giving God the glory that already belongs to Him by virtue of who He is. Biblical worship also focuses on God's infinite holiness.

False worship often involves immorality or ideas that are unworthy of God. But the true God is perfect in holiness, totally separated from sin. Worship that is worthy of Him must exalt and celebrate His purity.

Worship Has a Cost

Since God cares about the content of our worship, it shouldn't surprise us that He also cares deeply about the cost of our worship. In the book of Malachi, God rebuked His rebellious people for many things. But the first item on God's list was the shoddy, cheap worship that Israel was offering Him (1:6–14).

Instead of bringing God the best of their flocks for sacrifice, as His law demanded, the people were bringing Him their sick, blind, and lame animals. In other words, they were bringing that which was no great sacrifice.

"Offer it then to your governor! Would he be pleased with you?" God asked (Malachi 1:8). The answer was of course not. The Israelites wouldn't have offered a defective animal to an honored guest. That would have been an insult. Yet they were bringing God the worst they could find, and they weren't even embarrassed by it.

No wonder that God said, in effect, "Shut the doors of the temple so I won't have to put up with any more of these defective sacrifices. Stop your worship, because I won't accept it" (see Malachi 1:10). We must worship God in spirit and in truth, and that includes offering Him our very best.

Hebrews 13:15 calls our worship a "sacrifice" to God, reminding us that true worship always has a cost attached to it. When David went to buy the threshing floor from Ornan as the place to make a sacrifice (and upon which the temple of God would later be built), Ornan said, "Take it to yourself, and let my lord the king do what is good in his eyes" (1 Chronicles 21:23).

But David refused. "No, but I will surely buy it for the full price, for I will not take what is yours for the Lord, nor offer burnt offerings with that which costs me nothing" (v. 24). David would not settle for cheap worship, and neither can we.

WORSHIP HAS NO TIME LIMITS

Worship is a way of life for the authentic worshiper. "I will bless the Lord *at all times*" (Psalm 34:1, italics added). "From the rising of the sun to its going down the Lord's name is to be praised" (Psalm 113:3).

Worship is appropriate at any time and under any circumstance. "In everything give thanks; for this is the will of God in Christ Jesus for you" (1 Thessalonians 5:18).

Giving of Ourselves

I'm afraid that many of us only worship God when we feel like it or because of what we hope to get out of it. We come to church with the attitude *What am I going to get out of the music and the sermon today? How is coming to church going to make me feel better?*

But since we are the participants and not the spectators in worship, we need to ask what we can give to the worship service. The question is not what I get out of my worship, but what *God* gets out of it.

I realize there are times when we don't feel like worshiping. We wake up and say, "I'm not in the mood to worship," or, "I've got a headache and a cold, and I just don't think I can worship today."

Now if you're sick, you're sick. But whenever I start feeling this way about worship, I think of Job. In a matter of days, Job went from being the wealthiest man of his day to a childless, impoverished sufferer sitting on a garbage heap.

How did Job respond to his great losses? "Job arose,

tore his robe, and shaved his head; and he fell to the ground and worshiped. And he said . . . 'The Lord gave, and the Lord has taken away; blessed be the name of the Lord'" (Job 1:20–21). Job praised and worshiped God through his pain.

Please don't misunderstand. What we get from worship does matter. We need to draw truth, comfort, and encouragement from the Word and to be equipped for service. But the first question we should always ask is whether we have given ourselves to God in worship, expressing our love and devotion to Him and blessing Him.

Turning Hard Times into Worship

When you have this mind-set, you can truly worship God at all times and in all settings. We don't think much about the circumstances that John the apostle had to endure when he was exiled to the island of Patmos. But he was an old man, probably broken in health and completely cut off from his friends.

One day, however, John "was in the Spirit on the Lord's Day" on Patmos (Revelation 1:10), worshiping God. It was in that spirit of worship that he was given a glimpse of glory —and the result was the book of Revelation. When John entered into that magnificent worship service, he was lifted into the very presence of God.

Anyone can show up for church and enter into worship when things are going well. But the Christian praises God even in the hard times.

Paul and Silas were thrown into prison for preaching the gospel in Philippi. They were severely beaten and locked up in a filthy hole called a prison, and yet these two men decided that midnight was a great time for a praise and worship service (Acts 16:23–25). God enjoyed their worship so much that He shook the place and set them free. But the spirits of Paul and Silas were free long before those prison doors were jarred open. When you're in God's presence, you're always liberated. "Where the Spirit of the Lord is, there is liberty" (2 Corinthians 3:17).

God responds when His people determine to worship Him at all times. The result of this "prison ministry" was the salvation of the Philippian jailer (Acts 16:27–34). Because the apostles worshiped instead of whining about their circumstances, God turned their pain into a pulpit from which to proclaim the gospel.

WORSHIP BRINGS INCREDIBLE RESULTS

Worshiping God changes everything for us. He is listening and looking for people who continually and faithfully worship Him: people who sing songs in the night, who praise Him through prison bars, and who worship Him in spirit and in truth.

David wrote, "My soul shall make its boast in the Lord; the humble shall hear of it and be glad. Oh, magnify the Lord with me, and let us exalt His name together" (Psalm 34:2–3).

These verses suggest several benefits of worship. First, through our worship God the Father is magnified. We've learned that glorifying God is the first order of worship.

In worship our fellowship is unified. We are never closer to each other as believers than when we are together praising and worshiping God. The way to keep churches and families unified is to bring them together in the worship of Jesus Christ. Worship unifies the fellowship.

Worship fortifies our faith. "I sought the Lord, and He heard me, and delivered me from all my fears" (Psalm 34:4). Expressing adoration to God draws you nearer to Him. The Bible says that God inhabits the praises of His people (see Psalm 22:3). When you begin to praise God, your faith is lengthened, strengthened, and deepened.

Faith also clarifies your focus and edifies your future. "They looked to Him and were radiant, and their faces were not ashamed" (Psalm 34:5). We are not disappointed when we look to the Lord, because we can be assured that He will ultimately deliver us.

It's hard for life to get out of focus when your focus is fixed on Christ. "Keep your eyes on Him" is the Bible's advice to us (see Hebrews 12:2).

When we worship God authentically, the benefits are tremendous. "You will show me the path of life; in Your presence is fullness of joy; at Your right hand are pleasures forevermore" (Psalm 16:11).

Does that sound like the place you want to be? Then become an authentic worshiper of God.

NOTES

1. Donald Bloesch, "Whatever Happened to God?" *Christianity Today,* 5 February 2001, 54–55.
2. "The Heart of Worship" © 1999 by Kingsway's Thankyou Music (PRS). All rights administered in the Western Hemisphere by EMI Christian Music Publishing. All rights reserved. Used by permission.

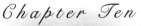

Chapter Ten

THE
REASON
WE WORSHIP

$\mathcal{S}$oon after it was launched by a space shuttle in 1990, the Hubble Space Telescope inspired a lot of derision and jokes when scientists discovered an error in the curvature of its lens. The result was blurred images transmitted back to earth. But a space walk by astronauts corrected the problem, and the huge telescope began doing what it was designed to do. The volume and the quality of Hubble's images are said to be astounding.

One scientist was even quoted as saying that he found it to be "a religious experience looking at the beauty of creation" through the images that Hubble transmits as it looks deep into space and reports what it sees.

There's an interesting correlation between what the Hubble telescope is designed to do and our task as believers in Jesus Christ. We are called to look deeply into the face of Jesus and then go and tell the world what we have seen as we reflect Jesus to those who don't know Him.

The first assignment is accomplished by our worship,

as we behold the face of Christ and are transformed in His presence. Worship sets our hearts on fire, as testified by the two disciples who met the risen Christ on the Emmaus road. Their response to being with Jesus was, "Did not our heart burn within us while He talked with us on the road?" (Luke 24:32).

Our second assignment, telling the world what we have seen, is accomplished by our witness. The Bible demonstrates that worship also leads to witness, the desire to tell someone else what we have seen and heard in God's presence. Once the Emmaus disciples' hearts were set on fire in Jesus' presence, they couldn't wait to tell someone else about the risen Christ (Luke 24:33–35).

Worship exalts Jesus Christ and gives Him His rightful place of pre-eminence in our lives. But it doesn't stop there. We come to know Christ in worship, and then we make Him known by proclaiming the good news of the gospel to the world.

So there comes a time when we get up from our knees, leave the place of worship, and enter the mission field. We gather to worship, then go out to witness. We gather to praise, then go out to proclaim. "To know Him and to make Him known" is the reason we worship. It could be the motto of every Christian's life, as it was for the apostle Paul. Paul's deepest desire in his relationship with Jesus Christ was "That I may know Him" (Philippians 3:10). He also affirmed of Christ, "Him we preach, warning every man and teaching every man in all wisdom" (Colossians 1:28). Because Paul spent time in the Lord's presence, he was energized and equipped to carry out his ministry of taking Christ to a lost world.

When you spend time with Jesus, revolutionary things happen. One of the most exciting examples of this in the Bible is found in Acts 4, where the enemies of the gospel were forced to recognize the power of Christ.

This power was being displayed in the lives of Peter

and John, who had healed a crippled man (Acts 3) and were courageously witnessing for Christ against all obstacles. Acts 4:1–14 tells how their witness brought Peter and John before the Sanhedrin, the ruling Jewish council in Jerusalem, whose members were amazed by the apostles' defense at a brief hearing.

Luke, the writer of Acts, described what happened next. "When they [the council] saw the boldness of Peter and John, and perceived that they were uneducated and untrained men, they marveled. And they realized that they had been with Jesus" (v. 13).

There was only one reason that Peter and John had such power, courage, and conviction: They had been with Jesus, and their lives were never the same again. We need the same balance of authentic worship and dynamic witness in our lives today—and it only comes from being with Jesus.

BEING WITH JESUS WILL
REVOLUTIONIZE YOUR LIFE

You may want to underline or mark the last part of Acts 4:13 in your Bible. The best thing anybody could ever say about you or me is that we have been with Jesus. What happens when you begin spending time with the living Lord of glory?

You'll Have an Unmistakable Resemblance to Jesus

It's impossible to spend any length of time in the presence of Jesus Christ and not demonstrate a spiritual resemblance to Him.

Peter and John had been with Jesus during His earthly ministry, walking and talking and living with Him for at least three years. They heard Him teach about the kingdom of God, listened to Him pray, and watched as He healed sick people and dealt with sinful people.

These two apostles had also been with Jesus in the Garden of Gethsemane, seeing His tears and agony of spirit (Matthew 26:36–46). And it was Peter and John who went to the empty tomb and became the first apostolic witnesses of the Lord's resurrection (John 20:1–10). The apostles were fully convinced that Jesus was alive, and they so clearly reflected His Person and His power that even their enemies had to admit the resemblance.

I wonder if the world would be forced to look at us and say, "We don't understand what it is that these people have, but it's obvious they've been with Jesus." Unsaved people aren't likely to study the Bible or come to church to gather firsthand research on us so they can figure us out. They simply watch us closely as we interact with friends, family, and business associates in the everyday world.

In other words, people will know if we've been with Jesus by our lives. That's how the apostles were identified as people who belonged to Christ.

Now in case you think revolutionary Christianity is only for apostles and other "super saints," let me remind you that there was nothing humanly extraordinary about the twelve men Jesus chose. They were living very simple lives when He called them.

In fact, these men were very ordinary, unlikely candidates for greatness. Someone has given us a humorous idea of what might have happened if Jesus had submitted their names to professional career consultants in Jerusalem to determine their qualifications for ministry:

> Thank you for submitting the résumés of the twelve men you are considering for management positions in your new organization. All of them have taken our battery of tests, the results of which we have run through our sophisticated computer analysis. We have also arranged personal interviews for each candidate with our psychologist and vocational aptitude consultant.

It is our staff's unanimous opinion that most of the nominees are lacking in qualification for the type of enterprise you are undertaking. We recommend that you continue your search for people of experience and managerial ability and proven capability.

We find that Simon Peter is emotionally unstable and given to fits of temper. He seems far too impulsive to be in a position of oversight. Andrew has absolutely no qualities of leadership.

The brothers James and John place personal interest above company loyalty, and they seem to be impatient with others. Due to this impatience and ambition they could one day become disgruntled employees.

Thomas demonstrates a questioning attitude that could tend to undermine morale. We feel it is our duty to tell you that Matthew has been blacklisted by the Greater Jerusalem Better Business Bureau.

In closing, one of the candidates shows great potential. He is a man of ability, resourcefulness, and ambition. We recommend Judas Iscariot as your controller and right-hand man. All the other profiles are self-explanatory.

> Sincerely yours,
> Jordan Management Consultants, Jerusalem

We tend to believe that the apostles and the other men and women who followed Jesus in those first days of the church were superhuman figures who stepped right out of stained-glass windows, and that's why God was able to use them so mightily. But this fictional report reminds us that the apostles were people of flaws and failures. The only thing that made them great was the time they spent with Jesus Christ.

The fact is that God loves to use ordinary people like you and me. Paul told the church at Corinth, "You see your calling, brethren, that not many wise according to the flesh, not many mighty, not many noble, are called" (1 Corinthians 1:26).

It's possible for any believer to look and act so much like Jesus that even people who don't know Him can't miss the resemblance. Don't insult God by saying He can't use you. God will use anyone who is available, expendable, and usable.

You'll Have Undeniable Fruit in Your Service

When you spend time with Jesus, other people will be attracted by the beauty and power of Christ, and pretty soon you won't be standing for Him alone. That's what happened to Peter and John at their first appearance before the Jerusalem council. Besides the testimony of the apostles' own lives, the council members were confronted with the undeniable evidence of the man Peter and John had healed at the Beautiful gate of the temple (Acts 3:2). Luke recorded the unfolding scene:

> And seeing the man who had been healed standing with them, they [the council] could say nothing against it. But when they had commanded them to go aside out of the council, they conferred among themselves, saying, "What shall we do to these men? For, indeed, that a notable miracle has been done through them is evident to all who dwell in Jerusalem, and we cannot deny it." (Acts 4:14–16)

Someone has said that if you're on fire for the Lord Jesus Christ, other people will be attracted by the flame and come to watch you burn. The fire comes from being with Jesus, beholding His face, and communing with Him in worship. Worship ignites our witness, giving it a power and authority we could never have if we tried to serve the Lord and win others in our own strength.

Jesus promised that if we would abide in Him, we would bear "much fruit" (John 15:5). The responsibility for fruit-bearing is His, not ours.

The formerly crippled man who accompanied Peter and John to their hearing before the Sanhedrin was Exhibit A of their ministry. According to Acts 4:22, he was "over forty years old" when the miracle occurred.

This was an interesting piece of evidence, for at least two reasons. First, it told everyone that this man was far too old simply to have "outgrown" his ailment. Second, he had been crippled his whole life and was a daily fixture among the beggars outside the temple (Acts 3:2). So anyone could easily verify that he had been in this condition for a very long time.

This man's healing was, by the Jewish council's own testimony, "a notable miracle" (4:16). And he was only one of a flood of people who turned to Christ as a result of the apostles' ministry. Three thousand were saved at Pentecost (Acts 2:41), and five thousand men came to Christ after Peter's sermon in response to this miraculous healing (4:4).

The fruit of our ministry may not be as spectacular as this, but that isn't our responsibility. When we spend time with Jesus, abiding in His presence, the fruit will come.

You'll Have the Unimaginable Power of the Spirit

There's a real temptation in reading these exciting accounts from the church's early days. The temptation is to go charging out and try to win the world for Jesus Christ without first spending the necessary time with Him.

But the order is all-important. Being with Jesus, coming to know Him and wait on Him in worship, always precedes effective ministry for Him. The early church provides us with a classic example of God's order in service.

Before Jesus sent Peter, John, and the other disciples charging into the world with the gospel, He gave them this command: "Tarry in the city of Jerusalem until you are endued with power from on high" (Luke 24:49), referring to the promised coming of the Holy Spirit.

The Lord issued this command on the day of His resurrection, and He repeated it just before His ascension. "He commanded them not to depart from Jerusalem, but to wait for the Promise of the Father, 'which,' He said, 'you have heard from Me; for John truly baptized with water, but you shall be baptized with the Holy Spirit not many days from now'" (Acts 1:4–5).

So those first believers waited and worshiped (Acts 2:1), and the Holy Spirit baptized them with His presence and His power exactly as Jesus had promised.

There is unimaginable power available to us in the Person of the Holy Spirit, who lives within each one of us. The early church became engaged in a full-time ministry of taking the gospel to the world, and these believers shook the world for Christ (see Acts 17:6).

The same thing can happen to us when we come before the Lord, worshiping Him and opening our lives to be filled with the Holy Spirit (Ephesians 5:18). But we can't reverse God's order of presence before power. And we can't substitute anything else for God's presence or power.

I fear that too few churches and believers today are depending solely upon the power of the Holy Spirit for ministry. We rely upon entertainment, human energy, programs, or gimmicks in an attempt to impact the world.

The New Testament church had nothing but this promise of Jesus to depend upon: "You shall receive power when the Holy Spirit has come upon you; and you shall be witnesses to Me in Jerusalem, and in all Judea and Samaria, and to the end of the earth" (Acts 1:8).

God gave us the Holy Spirit so that we might be infused with divine power to take the gospel to the world. We can be courageous and confident when we are filled with and controlled by the Holy Spirit.

The purpose of worship is that we may spend time with God and allow the Holy Spirit to fill us. The Spirit's filling happens again and again as we come before the

Lord, because our human vessels "leak" and we need to be continually renewed.

The Holy Spirit's job is not simply to give us exciting times of worship and "feel good" experiences. Some people are more interested in the *feeling* of the Spirit than they are in the *filling* of the Spirit. We have the unimaginable power of the Spirit to help us become effective witnesses for Christ.

You'll Have an Unquenchable Passion for Souls

When you've been with Jesus, your heart will burn with a passion for lost souls.

As a pastor, I am often asked interesting questions. For example, "Pastor, when is our church going to stop growing and expanding?" The answer to that is never. As long as there is one person in our community, or around the world, who needs to receive Jesus Christ as Savior and become His disciple, the church's task is unfinished. Our mission, given to us by Christ Himself, is to "make disciples" until He returns (Matthew 28:19). But until our mission becomes our passion, we won't take it very seriously.

Another question I'm asked is, "Pastor, don't you think the church should just slow down a little bit on outreach and grow the people we already have?" Let me tell you, the best way to grow people up *in* Christ is to send them out as personal witnesses *for* Christ.

Now of course, new believers need teaching and nurturing, and the church provides for these. But let's not allow anything to quench our passion for souls. Jesus said, "Follow Me, and I will make you fishers of men" (Matthew 4:19).

If we're followers, we'll become fishers! Jesus was so passionate about reaching lost people that He sought out sinners like Zacchaeus for salvation. The Lord explained His actions by saying, "The Son of Man has come to seek and to save that which was lost" (Luke 19:10).

Spiritual growth results in a burning desire to share Christ. When we're doing the job God called us to do, that's when we're growing the most and when we become more and more like our Savior who came to save the lost.

The best witness is a person who has experienced the presence and the power of Jesus Christ. When you have been with Jesus, when you have worshiped Him in spirit and in truth, you can't wait to tell somebody else.

The Samaritan woman who met Jesus at Jacob's well couldn't wait to run back into the city of Sychar and tell everyone she met about Jesus Christ (John 4:29). The man delivered from a legion of demons went back home and told all that Jesus had done for him (Mark 5:20).

When you've been with Jesus, you can't help but become passionate about sharing His grace with others.

BEING WITH JESUS WILL REALIGN YOUR LOYALTIES

We generally admire people who stand by what they believe and are loyal to their cause, regardless of the cost. The stand that Peter and John made before the Jewish council in Jerusalem indicates how completely loyal they were to their Lord.

You'll Have a Fearless Devotion to Christ

If you have been with Jesus in the secret place of worship, you'll be loyal to Him in the public square—even when people try to intimidate you into silence.

Following their brief examination of Peter and John, the members of the Sanhedrin decided to stop this burgeoning "Jesus movement" before it got out of hand (Acts 4:16–17). They thought they could threaten the apostles into keeping quiet, and it would all be over.

So they called Peter and John back into the council chamber and said, "Don't ever teach or speak again in the name of Jesus" (see v. 18). The implied threat of punishment was real, and in fact the apostles were later beaten severely for preaching about Christ (Acts 5:40).

Can you imagine the council ordering Peter and John never to mention Jesus again? They might as well have commanded the sun to stop shining. For the apostles, the issue of their loyalty had already been settled. They were fearless because they knew they belonged to Christ, and they knew He would not fail them.

So Peter and John answered the council, "Whether it is right in the sight of God to listen to you more than to God, you judge. For we cannot but speak the things which we have seen and heard" (Acts 4:19–20). The council threatened them again (v. 21), but they were undeterred.

The apostles and many other early believers were loyal to Christ to the death. We know from Scripture that the apostle James was killed by Herod (Acts 12:1–2). Church tradition reports that Matthew was also killed by the sword. Philip was hanged. Andrew, the gentle brother of Peter who was always bringing people to Jesus, was crucified and preached Jesus to all who walked by as he hung dying. Thomas was killed with a spear. And Peter was crucified upside down at his own request, for he felt unworthy to be crucified in the same way Jesus was crucified. Only the apostle John lived to a ripe old age, and he was exiled to the island of Patmos for preaching Jesus.

When you spend time with Jesus, you'll cultivate a devotion to Him that no power on earth can break.

You'll Have a Fierce Determination to Witness

If a law were passed today making it a crime to speak about Jesus, would it change anything in your life?

For some of us, it has been a long time since we talked to anybody about Jesus. It has been a long time since our neighbors or co-workers heard us mention His name. The apostles said they couldn't possibly stop teaching and preaching about Jesus. They were determined to be His witnesses even if it cost their lives. How fierce is your determination to tell others about Christ?

Surveys show that 95 percent of professing Christians have never led another person to faith in Christ. Some people will object that they just don't know any lost people. Those same surveys indicate that on average, every Christian knows between eight and nine people who do not know Jesus Christ. They're all around us in our circle of influence. Someone you know needs to know Jesus. And if you don't know anyone who isn't already in the body, how can you expand your circle to get to know some unbelievers?

Peter and John were bold witnesses because they had been with Jesus. Could it be that the reason we don't witness about our faith to others is that we're not spending time with the Lord in worship and adoration and praise? How can we say that we love and serve Christ, and yet never open our mouths to tell anyone else about Him?

Telling others about Jesus is not complicated. Peter and John were said to be "uneducated and untrained men" (Acts 4:13), meaning that they had not been to the recognized rabbinical schools of the day. They were laborers, but God used them because they had been with Jesus.

One of the simplest and most effective ways to share Christ is to follow the examples we find in the Scripture. After Jesus called the apostle Philip to follow Him, Philip went to tell his friend Nathanael he had found the Messiah (John 1:43–45). But Nathanael was skeptical: "'Can anything good could come out of Nazareth?' Philip said to him, 'Come and see'" (v. 46).

The woman at the well said the same thing to the people in her town: "Come [and] see" (John 4:29).

If you know Christ, you can say to your neighbors and friends, "Come and see—come and meet Jesus for yourself." I encourage you to begin praying specifically for the people living around you, and get to know them and let them know of your concern. Prayer will turn to concern for your neighbors.

No threats or intimidation can keep a Spirit-filled Christian from telling of the love of Jesus Christ. You can talk about Jesus in the normal daily patterns of your life. If you will witness, you'll soon discover what Paul discovered: "I am not ashamed of the gospel of Christ, for it is the power of God to salvation for everyone who believes" (Romans 1:16).

In this same account in Acts 4, we have a very important principle for our witness. Telling the world about Christ is so foundational to ministry that even if the highest authorities should order us to stop, we cannot (Acts 4:19–20). For Peter and John, it was an issue of Christ's lordship in their lives. The reason we witness, the reason we serve, and the reason we worship is because of love for Jesus Christ. We cannot help but speak about the One who is our life.

The religious establishment of the first century sought to stop the Christian message but could not. The mighty Roman Empire could not eradicate the Christian faith. Where is the Roman Empire today? Rome is a city of dead relics and ancient ruins—a tourist destination. The Caesars who demanded total loyalty from their subjects, and who were worshiped as gods, are buried in the dust of history.

But people whose total loyalty is to Jesus Christ are still worshiping Him and then going out to tell the world about Him. Are you spending time with the Lord? Have you been with Jesus? Then you have something to share that the world needs desperately.

Chapter Eleven

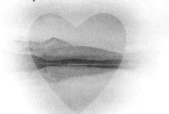

A HEART
FOR LOST
PEOPLE

I don't think I have met anyone with more of a heart for the Lord and for people than my friend Bobby Richardson, who was a key member of the great New York Yankees' teams of the 1950s and 60s.

Bobby has such a deep commitment to ministry that he retired from baseball after the 1966 season to give his time to the Lord's work, although he was only thirty-one and at the peak of his career.

When the Yankees gave Bobby a special day in his honor, he made sure that evangelistic tracts containing his testimony were distributed at Yankee Stadium that day. One New York sportswriter commented that God shared the spotlight on "Bobby Richardson Day."

Bobby's witness among his teammates was so strong that when the Yankee great Mickey Mantle entered a Dallas hospital in 1995 and learned he was dying of liver cancer, he called Bobby.

Bobby told me in a later conversation how he and his

wife came to Dallas immediately and shared the gospel with Mickey Mantle in his hospital room. Mantle responded, and Bobby had the joy of leading his old friend and ex-teammate to faith in Jesus Christ just a few days before Mantle died.

The story that Bobby related to me was later published in a gospel tract telling the dramatic story of Mickey Mantle's deathbed conversion. That tract is still in print and pointing people to Christ.

We're amazed when we hear of a person like Bobby Richardson who gives up something of great earthly value, such as a successful career, in order to devote his time to reaching others for the Lord.

But the fact is that all of us have been called and commissioned to be Christ's witnesses. A heart that is deeply in love with Jesus, and longs to know Him and live obediently under His lordship, is also a heart that loves lost people and beats with a desire to see them come to faith. When we get to heaven, what will matter is the investments we have made in bringing other people with us.

To become a vital part of our Christian lives, our evangelism has to come from the heart. We need to have compassion for those who don't know the Lord and a passion to see them come to faith in Christ.

How can we develop a passionate heart for lost people? To help answer that question, I want us to look into the heart of a person with such a passion for souls that he wrote, "I could wish that I myself were accursed from Christ for my brethren, my countrymen according to the flesh."

You may recognize that statement as coming from the pen and the heart of the apostle Paul, perhaps the greatest Christian who ever lived. Paul's unusual wish is recorded in Romans 9:3, right in the middle of a section of Scripture (9:1–5) in which he poured out his heart's desire for the salvation of his fellow Jews. Paul's example has a lot to teach us about what it means to have a heart for people.

OUR COMPASSION HAS TO BE REAL

Compassion can't be counterfeited. We can't fake concern for lost people if we don't feel it. Paul could write with deep conviction, "I tell the truth in Christ, I am not lying, my conscience also bearing me witness in the Holy Spirit, that I have great sorrow and continual grief in my heart" (Romans 9:1–2).

Paul was part of the family of Israel, and he greatly desired to see God's chosen people come to know Jesus Christ as their Messiah. His concern was well-founded. Since the earliest days of the church until today, most of the Jewish people have rejected Jesus. Paul saw this in his own ministry, and his heart was breaking for Israel.

The apostle also had a burden for the world, which propelled him out beyond the borders of Israel to share Christ with the people across his world. Paul had one message, the Cross of Christ, and he preached it everywhere he went.

Never Get over a Desire for God's Heart

When our compassion for people is real, no one will have to prompt and push us to tell them the good news of Jesus Christ. Our heart needs to reflect God's heart, which is continually open to those who are separated from Him.

Peter said that God is "not willing that any should perish but that all should come to repentance" (2 Peter 3:9). Our Father is so concerned for the lost that He is withholding judgment to give unsaved people more opportunities to repent.

We tend to think of Paul as "Super Saint," with the rest of us down the line somewhere. But let's not kid ourselves. Paul's passion for lost people is supposed to be the norm, not the exception. If we don't have a consuming burden for lost people and a passion to tell them about Christ, our spiritual lives are seriously deficient.

I wonder if our hearts could stand up under the searchlight Paul turned on himself concerning his desire to see people saved. "I'm not making this up or exaggerating," he was saying. "This is not religious jargon. I'm not saying this because I'm an apostle or a preacher. Let the Holy Spirit examine my heart and confirm that I have great and continual sorrow over those who don't know Jesus Christ" (see Romans 9:1–2).

We can never be casual or careless about the needs of people around us. We can't afford to become so comfortable in our pews that we simply watch the world pass by us. What will keep our hearts tender toward the lost men and women we meet at work, at school, or in our own families and neighborhoods? I see at least two factors in Paul's life that we can learn from.

Never Get over Getting Saved

The problem with many of us Christians is that we got saved, but then we got over it. Not Paul. He never recovered from the realization that God had reached down in grace and saved him. On one occasion, Paul said he was compelled to be a witness by the love of Christ (see 2 Corinthians 5:14). He wasn't speaking of his love for Christ at that point, but Christ's love for him. Paul was so overwhelmed by God's love for him that he spent the rest of his life telling others what Jesus had done for him and how they could know Him.

We must never forget what God had to do to save us. Some of us may have been "upstanding" sinners before we were saved, but we were completely lost and cut off from God. Peter said that when we forget that we were "cleansed from [our] old sins," we become spiritually shortsighted (2 Peter 1:9).

If you have personally encountered the living Christ and experienced His love in salvation, it should be the natural and normal course of your life to tell others about Him. Salvation is not an experience you have at one time, and then get over.

Besides securing your eternal destiny, your salvation should be the beginning point of your commissioning and empowering as a witness for the Lord. The Holy Spirit lives within every believer, and His work is to enable and equip us for the ministry of telling others about Jesus Christ.

Jesus said, "Follow Me, and I will make you fishers of men" (Matthew 4:19). Witnesses simply tell what they have seen or heard or what happened to them. You can see this often in the book of Acts. The apostles built their witness around their personal experience with Christ. Paul did this in his defense before King Agrippa (Acts 26).

The reason a lot of Christians aren't witnessing is that they haven't seen very much, heard very much, or had very much happen to them. The apostles told the Jerusalem leaders, "We cannot but speak the things which we have seen and heard" (Acts 4:20).

If our lives don't have that sense of urgency and passion that says, "We can't help but talk about what Jesus has done for us and what He can do for you," we ought not to get off of our knees until we get it. Don't get over your salvation.

Never Get over the Fate of the Lost

When was the last time we wept, prayed, or fasted for souls who are mortgaged to the devil? The answer to that question will go a long way toward telling us whether we truly have a heart for the lost.

Paul's burden for souls was prompted by his own conversion. But it was also propelled by his compassion for the fate of those who were without Christ. He said that his sorrow for Israel's lost condition was "great" and "continual"

(Romans 9:2). He was grief-stricken at the possibility of people spending an eternity separated from God in the torment of hell.

The Bible says that Jesus "was moved with compassion" as He looked out over the people, "because they were weary and scattered, like sheep having no shepherd" (Matthew 9:36).

The Lord experienced deep emotion over the people's lost condition—and notice His response. "The harvest truly is plentiful, but the laborers are few. Therefore pray the Lord of the harvest to send out laborers into His harvest" (vv. 37–38). Jesus called for witnesses who felt the same heartbreaking burden for people that He felt.

The Savior also wept over Jerusalem as He approached the city in His triumphal entry on the way to the cross (Luke 19:41). The word used here to describe Jesus' weeping is not simply the trickling of a few tears down the face, but great heaving sobs as God Himself wept over a city full of lost souls whom He loved and longed to draw to Himself.

Dr. Stephen Olford, a great preacher in his own right, tells about being with Billy Graham in New York for a crusade back in the 1950s. Dr. Olford was standing with Billy Graham as they looked out over the city, and he said that Graham's shoulders began to shake and his body began to quiver as he wept over that great city filled with people who needed Christ.

Is it any wonder that God has used Billy Graham to proclaim the gospel to the ends of the earth, given that he has a heart and a compassion for people like that? If we're going to reach people for the Lord and make a difference in this generation, we need to ask for a burden for souls that is so deep it will erupt in tears at times.

If you want a remarkable modern-day example of a passion for souls, you'll find one in a most unlikely place— the city dump on the outskirts of Cairo, Egypt.

Cairo is a huge city of 18 million people, many of whom are trapped in staggering poverty. Some 50,000 people actually live at the Cairo dump, somehow eking out an existence on the trash from the rest of the city. The living conditions and the stench in this place are said to be unbearable. But right in the middle of all this poverty and suffering is a thriving Christian church.

The story of this amazing church is that, in 1972, an Egyptian garbage collector who was a believer began witnessing of Christ with one of the people living in the dump. It wasn't too long before this garbage collector sensed God was calling him to move into the dump and minister to these people.

Like Jonah, this man was repelled at the idea at first, and he got on a bus going in the opposite direction. But he came under conviction, switched buses, gathered up all of his belongings, and moved into the dump with these people despised by society to win them to Christ.

An American Christian leader who recently visited this "church at the dump" in Cairo said it now has more than five thousand people in attendance weekly. All because one individual cared more about eternal souls than about his temporary comfort. Have we become so comfortable that we don't notice a world around us plunging headlong into hell?

This same Christian leader said he met a pastor last year who flies to Washington, D.C., every week at his own expense to walk the streets of our nation's capital and pray for revival as he sheds tears over America's spiritual needs.

You and I may not fly to Washington to walk the streets and weep over souls. But we can walk the streets of our neighborhoods and our cities with our hearts breaking for lost souls, pleading with God for a mighty movement of His hand. The only question is: Do we care enough to do so?

OUR PASSION HAS TO BE CONSISTENT

One of our problems today is that we run hot and cold for Christ. We hear a stirring message, or we see a critical need, and our hearts are moved. We catch fire for the Lord for a while, but then the flames cool to embers and die out.

It's a common problem, and I admit that I struggle with it at times just as you do. We need a heart that beats continually and consistently for the lost. Paul testified that his burden for his fellow Jews was constant. "I have ... continual grief in my heart" (Romans 9:2).

In other words, Paul's passion for people wasn't something that just hit home with him every so often and stirred his heart. It was literally a way of life for this apostle.

It was said of the early church that they were about the work of Christ continually (see Acts 2:42–47). In terms of their witness, all of them were at it, and they were at it all the time. They never let up or backed up. They kept moving forward with the gospel.

This is the kind of spiritual passion I want, and I believe you do too. How do we maintain the fire in our own hearts? How do we stay constant and consistent in our walk with the Lord and in our witness for Him?

Keep Praying at All Times

If you aren't praying regularly for lost people, and specifically for opportunities to witness to them, it is highly unlikely—in fact, I think it is impossible—for you to have a consistent burden for lost people.

I believe the secret of having a heart for the lost begins and ends with prayer. Time spent on our faces before God is the way to light the flame inside. Get alone with God and draw so near to Him that you can hear the beat of His heart, and your own heart will begin to beat with His heart.

Paul wrote, "Pray without ceasing" (1 Thessalonians 5:17). This is more than a command to the church. It gives us a glimpse into Paul's heart and helps us see what made him so consistent in his ministry. He prayed consistently.

Prayer and evangelism are like twin sisters in the Scriptures. After the apostles had been threatened by the Jewish leaders not to speak anymore in the name of Jesus, they went back to the church and reported what had happened.

Then the Bible says that the people "raised their voice to God with one accord" (Acts 4:24). What did they pray for? "Grant to Your servants that with all boldness they may speak Your word" (v. 29). And when they finished praying, the Holy Spirit shook the building, "and they spoke the word of God with boldness" (v. 31).

I don't believe we'll be consistent in our witness until we're consistent in prayer. Do you have a prayer list filled with the names of unsaved people you are bringing before the Lord regularly, asking for their salvation?

We know that God is not willing for anyone to perish, and that He delights to save. Jesus said He came to seek and save the lost (Luke 19:10).

If you don't have a deep, abiding burden for souls, ask God to give you one. If you find yourself cold and indifferent toward others, get alone with God and ask Him to move in your heart. Stay in prayer as long as it takes to light a flame in your heart—one that burns with the message of Christ and a desire to share that message with those who need it most.

You Can't Win Just One

Witnessing for Christ and winning others to Him is like the famous potato chip commercial that said, "You can't eat just one." If you have ever had the incredible joy of leading another person to Jesus Christ, you know that you can't win just one. Once you serve as a spiritual "midwife" in the birth of a new soul into God's family, you'll get excited and want to repeat the process again and again.

This is another way to keep your passion for souls alive and strong. Having prayed and prepared, go out and witness! There's nothing profound or mysterious about this. It's easy to become passionate about something when you're immersed in it.

Why shouldn't we get excited about bringing people to Christ? Heaven does. Jesus said that the angels in God's presence explode in heavenly praise and celebration when a sinner repents (see Luke 15:10).

I often wish that the people in our church could stand where I stand on Sunday morning as I give the invitation and see people come forward to receive Christ. Some of these new believers have been witnessed to and led to Christ by people in the church who have a heart for souls.

To stand there on the platform and see people getting saved is a joy beyond all other joys on earth. When you start discussing your faith with others and God uses you to win people to Christ, you will become so energized and excited that you won't need any external motivation to become a witness.

Warning People with Passion

If we believe what God's Word says about the hopeless future of those who are without Christ, we will be stirred to the depths of our being. The thought of even one individual spending eternity apart from God in hell is incomprehensible.

Paul said, "Knowing, therefore, the terror of the Lord, we persuade men" (2 Corinthians 5:11). Having a clear conviction from the Word of God about the certainty of His judgment will keep us going and growing in our witness.

To the apostle Paul, the prospect of God's judgment

was a terrifying thing that drove him to warn the lost and seek their salvation. This is not a groveling fear that makes us want to hide from God, but holy awe of the Lord in light of the fact that He will one day judge the world. The writer of Hebrews said, "It is a fearful thing to fall into the hands of the living God" (Hebrews 10:32).

But notice that it was Paul who felt "the terror of the Lord," not lost people. They should be afraid of standing before God, no doubt about it. But Paul was the one motivated by the awe-inspiring thought of God as the Judge. The apostle felt it was his responsibility to warn people and plead with them to receive the Lord.

We say we believe that men and women apart from Jesus Christ are without hope for eternity. If we believe this, then the terror of the Lord will also move us to do all we can to persuade unsaved people about the gospel.

We're not talking about self-effort in trying to win the lost, but telling of Christ with a sense of urgency. If you saw a building on fire and ran inside to warn the occupants, you wouldn't be casual about your warning. You would deliver your message with real passion, and you would insist that the people in the building believe you and act accordingly.

The Bible is clear that the judgment awaiting unsaved people is far worse than being trapped in a burning building. They are dangling on the edge of the abyss called hell, and only by faith in Jesus Christ can they be pulled back from that abyss. I'm very concerned about this because the most recent surveys show that an alarming number of people who say they are Christians don't believe in hell and eternal judgment.

These people can't bring themselves to believe that God will actually judge and condemn those who reject Christ. Too many people in the church don't know the God of the Bible. Instead, they know the cultural god of today, who is all love and life and sweetness.

The God of the Bible is certainly a God of love, and a

God of great grace and mercy. He loved us so much that He sent His only Son to die on the cross for us, to take our judgment upon Himself. But those who reject that love and refuse to let Christ take their judgment have nothing left but condemnation from God. Some who say they are Christians may not believe what the Bible teaches about eternal judgment—but if we believe it, we cannot keep quiet.

Faithfulness in prayer, constancy in our witness, and a conviction based on God's Word will help keep us consistent in our passions for souls.

THE "ILLOGIC" OF A PASSIONATE HEART

Are you willing to pay any price, to do whatever is necessary, to bring people to Jesus Christ? Paul said something amazing in Romans 9:3: "For I could wish that I myself were accursed from Christ for my brethren, my countrymen according to the flesh."

This is what I call the illogic of a passionate heart. Don't try to put logic to Paul's statement. He was speaking from the depths of a heart that was burdened for souls. He seemed to be saying that he would be willing to go to hell himself if it would mean salvation for his fellow Jews.

Paul couldn't do that, of course, but even saying he was willing gives us another tremendous insight into what it means to have a heart for unsaved people. Paul wasn't just being dramatic or overstating himself, because he called the Holy Spirit to be his witness that he was telling the truth (Romans 9:1–2).

The tragedy today is that the vast majority of Christians don't even try to win others to Christ. Surveys say that 85 percent of church members in America have never witnessed to an unbeliever. God help us to have the spirit of Paul, to do whatever necessary to bring people to Jesus.

It costs to reach people for Christ. It costs to have a heart that is broken for a world full of people heading toward an eternity without Christ. It will cost us time, effort, energy, and even money to be Christ's witnesses.

But when we love Christ and love people as Paul did, we will go beyond reason into the realm of sacrifice. Caring so much for lost people that you're willing to make any sacrifice may not seem logical to the world's way of thinking, but it makes perfect sense from the standpoint of God's kingdom!

With all the lessons of the heart that we have learned, let's make sure that our hearts are turned upward toward God and outward toward others. Proverbs 11:30 says, "He who wins souls is wise." I want to leave you with a special word of challenge.

During the 2001 national college basketball tournament, the Duke University Blue Devils faced the University of Maryland in a semifinal game. Duke and Maryland were two of the Final Four teams. The winner of the game would play for the national championship.

But in spite of the game's importance, Duke played poorly and fell behind by 22 points early in the first half. The team rallied a little but still went into the locker room at halftime trailing Maryland by 11 points.

When it was time for the teams to return to the court for the second-half warm-up, the Duke players stayed behind in the locker room. One by one, each player challenged his teammates with these words: "Find your heart."

Duke's players repeated this challenge to each other again and again, and the rest is history. Duke rallied to beat Maryland, then defeated the University of Arizona for the national title two nights later.

What a great challenge those words are to us. Because of our great God, and because of the calling we have to share His love and grace with the world, my closing challenge to you is this: Christian, find your heart!

Other titles from Moody Press:

The reality of heaven is the cord that keeps pulling us onward and upward in life. Yet, if eternity is not the habit of our heart, life soon becomes hollow and unsatisfying. The frantic pace and seductiveness of this present world threaten to blur our focus on eternity. We are left with a nagging sense of meaninglessness that haunts our souls.

ISBN# 0-8024-4153-X, Paperback, Christian Living

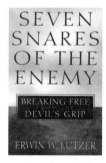

Opportunities to be ensnared by sin abound to-day. We live in a world filled with enticements that wait to trip us up and even reach out to us from the Internet, movies, television, and the world at large in an effort to pull us into their grasp. Many good people, even Christians, are caught by these snares—and one wrong decision can start a progression that results in destroyed lives.

ISBN#0-8024-1164-9, Paperback, Christian Living

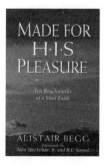

For many Christians, God the Father seems as distant as Jesus seems reachable. We wonder about how the Father sees us, what He wants from us. We recognize that we understand very little about His character. But to really know Him seems impossible. Yet nothing could be further from the truth.

ISBN#0-8024-3007-4, Paperback, Christian Living